D0567858

JEEP
COLOR HISTORY

First published iin 1999 by MBI Publishing Company, 729 Prospect Avenue, PO Box 1, Osceola, WI 54020-0001 USA

MBI Publishing Company books are also available at discounts in bulk quantity for industrial or sales-promotional use. For details write to Special Sales Manager at the Motorbooks International Wholesalers & Distributors, 729 Prospect Avenue, PO Box 1, Osceola, WI 54020-0001 USA.

Library of Congress Cataloging-in-Publication Data

Statham, Steve.
    Jeep color history / Steve Statham.
      p. cm.
    Includes index.
    ISBN 0-7603-0636-2 (pbk. : alk. paper)
    1. Jeep automobile—History. 2. Jeep automobile Pictorial works. I. Title.
    TL215.J44S73 1999
    629.222—dc21   99-27099

On the front cover: Two legendary members of an elite Jeep family pose side-by-side. The Jeep CJ-2A was the first civilian Jeep. It featured a side-mounted tire, a rear tailgate, and larger headlamps. It is an extremely hot commodity on the collector's market. This yellow 1948 CJ-2A is owned by Jim Geraci of Spring, Texas. An evolved CJ going by another name, Wrangler, appeared on the scene in 1987, and four or five variations of the model were typically available. This SE model first arrived in 1994. The luxury trim package was positioned one step above the entry-level "S" model. With full padding on the sport bar, 15x7 styled steel wheels with P215/75 R15 tires, rear bumperettes, a rear fold and tumble seat, and an AM/FM stereo, the offroad pioneer had been drastically refined from its early predecessors.

On the frontispiece: The creator of the Jeep, Willys-Overland, placed the stylized Willys "W" prominently on the Jeepster hood. These small touches gave the rugged Jeeps an added styling.

On the title page: The Jeep Utility Wagon was a crucial part of Jeep's postwar strategy to diversify its product line while playing on the Universal's reputation. From its 1946 introduction to its slow death in the mid-1960s, the wagon changed little over the years.

On the back cover: Top: Jeep was one of the originators of the sport utility movement, and the Grand Cherokee models now lead the charge. The Laredo occupied the middle ground in the Grand Cherokee pecking order, between the base and Limited models. Unique Grand Cherokee Laredo equipment included argent lower bodyside cladding with a black accent strip, argent fascias and bumper guards, a bright grille with argent inserts, 15x7 five-spoke wheels, and front bucket seats and door panels covered with "Barton/Bishop" cloth. *Jeep photo* **Bottom:** The vehicle that started the Jeep phenomenon was the World War II military Jeep. This is a M38A1 Jeep, which was put into production in 1951. The civilian version, the CJ-5, commenced in 1954. The hood cutout was for high-water snorkel equipment, which kept water from flooding the engine.

Edited by Paul Johnson
Designed by Dan Perry

Printed in Hong Kong

CONTENTS

ACKNOWLEDGMENTS

For a writer, embarking on a book project always involves more than just snapping photos and banging on a keyboard. And when it comes to chronicling 60 years of Jeep history, it takes a *whole* lot of help from Jeep enthusiasts, historians, collectors, and people who were there at the beginning. An awful lot of people cleared their calendars, set aside their work and gave of their free time to help me get the story down. I owe a whole truckload of thanks.

I'll start by thanking Rob Reaser, founding editor of *JP Magazine,* for his advice, tips, contacts, and a lot of magazine assignments through the years. Rob's enthusiasm for the subject was always infectious, and he introduced me to corners of the Jeep world I would never have found on my own. Thanks also to fellow book scribe Mike Mueller for his help in assembling material, but also for his steady encouragement.

Many people helped me dig up those musty old historical photos people love to see. Thanks to Anne Cook at the Texas Department of Transportation and the good folks at the Austin History Center, for allowing me to ransack their photo files in search of Jeep-related images. Others who proved instrumental in assisting my research, or helping me acquire the right photos include: Greg Pringle with the San Antonio Public Library; Mark Patrick at the Detroit Public Library National Automotive History Collection; Carolyn Wright at the U.S. Army Transportation Museum at Fort Eustis, Virginia; and General John C.L. Scribner at Camp Mabry, Austin, Texas. My father-in-law, Lt. Col. Bob Rice (ret.), helped point me in the right direction for my research at Fort Sam Houston in San Antonio.

Those who sat for interviews provided crucial insight into the Jeep's history. I'd especially like to thank Mark Smith, along with Jill and Greg Smith, at Jeep Jamboree USA. Chief Warrant Officer James Butcher (ret.), an MP for most of his military career, provided great first-hand memories of how the military Jeeps compared. Thanks also go to Jim Serr with the American Jeepster Club, who helped school me on Commando facts at 1997's American Jeepster Club reunion in Reno.

My own Wrangler has seen plenty of dirt under its wheels, but I've also spent a lot of time in passenger seats reporting on one off-road event or another. Long before I signed on to this book project, I was sent out into the field on magazine article assignments, and a number of Jeep clubs welcomed me with open arms. Some of the photography in this book comes from those events. So thanks to y'all in the Southwest Four-Wheel Drive Association, Jeep Exclusive of Amarillo, and the American Jeepster Club.

This certainly isn't the first book to chronicle the Jeep's history, nor will it be the last. Yet each has something unique to contribute. Many of these earlier titles were important sources of information and fact verification, and must be acknowledged. Jeep enthusiasts can put the following volumes on their reading lists and know when they turn the last page their understanding and appreciation of Jeep vehicles will be much more than it was before: *The Jeep—Its Development and Procurement under the Quartermaster Corps, 1940-1942,* by Herbert R. Rifkind; *Jeepers Jamboree Book II, The First 40 Years . . .,* by Peg Presba; *The Standard Catalog of Light Duty American Trucks, 1896-1986,* edited by John Gunnell; *Selling the All-American Wonder,* by Frederic L. Coldwell; *The Raiders; Desert Strike Force,* by Arthur Swinson; *Jeep, The Unstoppable Legend,* by Arch Brown;

The author's faithful Jeep, crossing the Sierra Nevada Mountain Range in 1995. Long highway cruises aren't the Wrangler's best use, but when the paved road ends, the Jeep just keeps going.

Jeep owners expect their vehicles to perform a numbers of tasks. Tom Sterlacci of Colorado owns the 1971 Jeepster Commando pictured. It has been with its owner for more than a quarter century, serving as college car and faithful companion, before being treated to a full restoration and custom camper. It is shown here at the American Jeepster Club reunion in Reno, Nevada, in 1997. Jeeps have become popular enough that even subdivisions down to specific models, like the Jeepster, can generate enough fans to support car clubs.

Beijing Jeep—The Short, Unhappy Romance of American Business in China, by Jim Mann; and *The Hurst Heritage*, by Robert C. Lichty and Terry Boyce. Certain production figures came from Motor Vehicle Manufacturers Association *Motor Vehicle Facts & Figures* volumes.

Many of the Jeeps photographed for this book came from a single collection, that of Jim and Peg Marski, of Pine, Colorado, and special thanks go to them. Our photo session lasted two days, through all kinds of iffy weather, but Jim was always of good cheer, and a good sport besides. Jim and Peg's vehicles include the 1950 Willys Jeep pickup, 1953 CJ-3B, 1962 Station Wagon, 1967 Jeepster convertible, 1970 CJ-5 Renegade I, 1971 Hurst Commando, 1972 V-8 Commando, and 1983 CJ-8. Long after I had packed my camera bags and moved on, Jim acquired yet more Jeeps, and volunteered to photograph them himself for use in this book. So Jim gets bonus thanks for providing photography of his 1964 Wagoneer and 1960 DJ-3A Surrey.

Many other Jeep owners graciously allowed me to photograph their vehicles and have my gratitude. These owners start with Mark Smith and the Jeepers Jamboree Museum in Georgetown, California. In their collection are the 1941 Willys MA and 1978 Expedicion de las Americas CJ-7 pictured herein. Thanks also go to: Col. Harry F. Rogers, Austin, Texas, 1942 Ford GPW; Steve Thrasher, Austin, Texas, 1942 Ford GPW with 1943 Willys GPT trailer (and a special thanks to former owner Milburn Locke for his generous help during our photo shoot); Don at Great Cars in Dallas, Steve McQueen Willys MB; Frank Guest, El Paso, Texas, 1949 Jeepster; Dorris and Russell "Rusty" Brown, El Paso, Texas, 1950 Jeepster; Matt and Judie Larsen, Plano, Texas, 1953 M38A1; Tom Sterlacci, Colorado, 1971 Commando with custom camper; Paul "Fuzzy" Winters, Hesperia, California, trail-equipped CJ-7 Renegade; Bert Beigel, Leander, Texas, 1979 DJ-5G postal Jeep; Patrick Stinson, Fort Worth, Texas, 1980 CJ-7 Renegade; Bob Norton with the South Western Four Wheel Drive Association (SWFWDA), XJ Cherokee; and Jeff and Jennifer Statham, Parker, Colorado, 1998 Cherokee Sport.

Finally, even though it will never read this, I'm nonetheless going to thank my own Jeep, my trusty 1994 Wrangler. My Wrangler is the best kind of Jeep—the *paid-for* kind. It is deserving of thanks for being utterly reliable during 115,000 miles worth of cross-country jaunts and off-road excursions. It has taken me to hidden Colorado ghost towns, to the Rio Grande River in Big Bend National Park, and survived the occasional Jamboree. It has been my workhorse on backcountry photo shoots, and has also been the only vehicle I've ever owned that has truly earned its keep. It has been the perfect vehicle for lazy softball Sundays. My wife may have married me for my Jeep (just kidding, sweetie, I think). No wonder people love these silly things.

Introduction

GLOBAL APPEAL

It is probably safe to say that the Jeep story is one of the most compelling in all of twentieth century automotive history. The Jeep saga has so many of the classic elements of traditional storytelling that it's a wonder the swashbuckling tale isn't told nightly as a bedtime story to wide-eyed children. The Jeep emerged from America's factories just in time to make a significant contribution to the nation's survival, thanks to men working under ferocious deadline pressure in the vehicle's creation. The Jeep survived the proving ground of global war, then rolled on through periods of worldwide fame, corporate death-battles, prosperity booms, and financial busts, along the way attracting vast hordes of admirers.

Of course, any bedtime story involving the Jeep will have its scary elements as well. There are the green-eyed monsters of greed and jealousy among corporations. There are the discomforts of the early Jeep's kidney-busting ride, negligible seats, and contortionist driving position. There have even been attacks by sometimes virulent quality control gnomes, plus the bogeymen of 22-mile-per-hour J-turns,

The traditional Jeep "face" has been transferred to all types of Jeep vehicles through the years, including station wagons, pickup trucks, and the Jeepster Commandos produced in the late 1960s and early 1970s. Although not produced in large numbers, the Commandos have developed a loyal following, as shown by this meeting of the American Jeepster Club in 1997.

Jeep owners are likely the most organized group in all "off-roaddom." Besides dozens of local Jeep Exclusive clubs, the Jeep Jamboree USA series of annual off-road excursions offers Jeep owners the chance to dirty their tires from coast-to-coast, and in a handful of foreign countries. The 1995 Texas Palo Duro Canyon Jamboree is pictured.

which resulted in the employment of vast hordes of a great many lawyers. So perhaps the story isn't suitable for children after all.

Despite, or perhaps because of, all of the above, the Jeep has become an American icon. It's one of those few products, like as Coca-Cola and Harley-Davidson motorcycles, that is instantly recognized worldwide as an American original. Did the legions of Jeep factory workers in Toledo, Ohio, know through the years that their efforts were producing rolling goodwill ambassadors for the United States?

As an icon the Jeep has not only been a war hero, but the subject of a feud, starting with the initial World War II–era fistfight between Willys and Ford for the right to call the Jeep its own. American Bantam, the company that built the first Jeep prototype, was knocked out in the first round. Willys won the battle to claim the Jeep name, but eventually sold out to Kaiser, which sold out to American Motors, which Chrysler then absorbed, so it's unclear who got the last laugh. Perhaps it's the millions of Jeep buyers through the years.

When giant corporations weren't fighting over the Jeep name, the Jeep as a product had its own fights against natural competitors in the automotive world. Through decades of marketplace battles, the Jeep has vanquished most of its direct competitors, although, ironically, its reward for winning resulted in the heightened industry-wide interest in the "sport utility" class of vehicles.

One of the earliest and most successful competitors of the Jeep was International Harvester's Scout, introduced in 1961. Designed in the classic Jeep mold, the Scout lasted until 1980. If International had managed to keep it in production until the sport utility boom of the late 1980s, it might have experienced a much different future.

Ford took a shot at the competition, too. The original small Ford Bronco was introduced for the 1966 model year, and took dead aim at both the Scout and the various small Jeep models in production. But Ford abandoned the compact sport utility field in 1978 to play against Chevy's full-size Blazer, which was introduced for 1969, only to return to the compact field with the Bronco II in 1983. While the basic Jeep Wrangler lives on, the Bronco II was put to pasture in favor of the Explorer, which was a response to the four-door Cherokee.

Although many of these early competitors are long gone, it's a testament to the Jeep's influence that today nearly every manufacturer plays in the Jeep's arena. Consumers can choose from an endless lineup of compact four-door utility vehicles, full-size land whales, and a wide variety of cute little sport-ute wannabes. Jeeps now compete against Blazers, Suburbans, Explorers, Expeditions, Excursions, Mountaineers, Navigators, Escalades, Denalis, Durangos, Pathfinders, Land Cruisers, Forerunners, Amigos, Sidekicks, Grand Vitaras, and Sportages. Some manufacturers such as Isuzu abandoned the passenger car market altogether in favor of the truck-making market. Venerable Land Rover even pulled its tail out from between its British legs, swam the pond, and staked a claim in the Jeep corner of the American market.

With over half the new vehicles sold in America now falling under the categories of light truck, minivan, or sport utility, it's fair to shower the Jeep with its share of the credit. Back in the early post–World War II days buyers in this segment had pretty much one choice—the Jeep. Most of the vehicles that followed came rumbling down the path the Jeep had blazed first.

Tracing the Appeal

What is it about this ill-riding, canvas-flapping, noisy little mule cart that has so thoroughly captured the imagination of the public?

Well, to start, Jeeps are a lot of fun.

Journalists and numerous Jeep owners have accurately stated that one perfect day in a Jeep, top down, crawling over some remote mountain pass, is worth putting up with the Jeep's shortcomings the other 364 days of the year. Fortunately, most people have more than one good Jeep day a year, but the appeal is clear. A Jeep is a specialized vehicle much the same as a high-revving sports car. It's not always ideal for everyday driving, but put it in its element and you've got pure driving pleasure.

Jeeps are escape machines. They take us to the wild places and remote areas that get harder to find with each passing year. The world grows more crowded and restrictions on the backcountry multiply daily, but we can still turn to this wonderful

Jeeps came crashing into America's consciousness thanks to the important role that they played in World War II. Created the year before the Japanese attack on Pearl Harbor, by war's end virtually everyone in the nation recognized the Jeep. Jeeps became an integral part of the military in a very short time span, as this November 1945 Armistice Day parade in Austin, Texas, shows. *Austin History Center, Austin Public Library*

Jeeps rarely stay in stock form for very long. Although Jeeps are capable performers straight from the factory, most enthusiasts immediately invest in larger wheels and tires for better ground clearance, as well as winches, locking differentials, CB radios, and various mounting racks and brackets designed to hold more camping gear. For some, Jeeps have become a way of life. Paul "Fuzzy" Winters of Hesperia, California (shown), has been four-wheelin' regularly since 1949.

machine, this sheet-metal pack mule, this motorized beast of burden to transport us to the secret trails that call out. In our Jeeps we are briefly nomads, carrying the bare essentials of life as we crisscross the world.

The Jeep has managed to maintain its integrity through time. It has stayed true to its roots. A GI from World War II stranded on a desert island for half a century would probably have no trouble identifying a 1998 TJ Wrangler as a Jeep, should he ever find his way back to civilization. (He'd probably get a hearty belly-laugh out of all the government-mandated or lawyer-recommended warning stickers affixed to the sun visors, glovebox door, jack, fan shroud, etc., ad nauseam.)

Over the years, the Jeep lineup has consisted of rugged, outdoorsy vehicles. There have been small utility off-road vehicles like the CJs, pickup trucks, and large four-wheel-drive utility wagons. But there have been no Jeep economy cars, sedans, or minivans. On the rare occasion when some oblivious product planner had the bright idea of affixing Jeep emblems to some AMC Hornet offspring or Dodge truck clone, sharper minds in the company veered away. Once diluted, a solid reputation is hard to restore. Therefore, Jeep has maintained a solid connection with its many fans by keeping its image and its product focus pure.

It's not that people never complain. Traditionally, die-hard Jeep aficionados are, at least initially, certain that each new Jeep is less capable than the last. The litany is familiar. The CJ-5s were never as good as the flat-fender models they replaced. The YJ Wrangler of 1987 was derided as a "Yuppie Jeep," not the legitimate heir to the CJ-7. Among the hard-core group, bumper stickers proclaiming that "Real Jeeps have round headlights" are still found. No doubt, there still exists a grizzled old soldier convinced the last good Jeep was the original Willys Quad prototype.

Such high standards among fans exist because Jeep enthusiasts love their vehicles, and live in fear that whichever corporation currently owns the Jeep brand will somehow screw up their favorite four-wheeled toy. What is remarkable is that the string of corporations that has owned the Jeep brand *hasn't* screwed up the basic concept. No other vehicle has maintained such closeness to its roots as the basic Jeep. A Wrangler is just as impractical and specialized a vehicle in today's world as any older CJ model was way back when, and every bit as capable off-road, if somewhat safer and more comfortable.

Even the high-end, full-luxury Jeep Grand Cherokees can match or exceed the rock-crawling talents of the older Wagoneers and Cherokees. They, too, maintain an honesty of design despite the fact that the top luxury models boast leather seats, cruise control, anti-lock brakes, air bags, and more computing power than that used to send the first men to the moon. The Grand Cherokees may have abandoned the simple leaf springs and hose-it-out interiors of the past, but they are expected to be able to crawl over mountaintops just as ably as earlier versions of the utility wagon. To this day, all new Jeep vehicles must be able to traverse California's challenging Rubicon Trail before receiving the sign-off for production.

One reason Americans have such a soft spot for Jeeps is because they have permeated so many aspects of everyday life. Jeeps have served as soldiers, farm hands, and good-time machines. They have even delivered our mail. Postal Jeeps, like this 1979 DJ-5G, can still occasionally be found in service on rural routes.

The Jeep's appeal extends far beyond the United States. In the Philippines, customized and flamboyantly decorated "Jeepneys" serve as taxicabs. Knockdown Mahindra Jeep kits in India have been produced from the immediate postwar per- iod into modern times. Surplus war Jeeps were sold throughout the United Kingdom, and British fans hold car shows celebrating these vehicles even today. Jeep has re-entered foreign markets around the world in recent years, most notably in Japan. It has also found a market in Australia, a country that sprang as a ready-made Jeep playground from the primordial oceans. The popular Jeep Jamboree USA series of off-road excursions has spread beyond U.S borders into Canada and Mexico.

Then and Now

Having survived all the struggles of the immediate postwar period, the Cold War, a handful of economic recessions, and scary 1970s-style inflation, the Jeep line, as of this writing, has cruised into its sixth decade in air-conditioned comfort. What challenges remain?

Besides the obvious challenge of defeating the new field of competitors in the marketplace, Chrysler has recently recognized the importance of encouraging brand loyalty in a new generation of Jeep owners. That new generation has many more sport utility vehicles to choose from than previous generations.

At the Chrysler-sponsored Camp Jeep, held annually in Colorado, new owners are taught how to drive in an off-highway environment, discovering in the process the capabilities of Jeep vehicles. The camp features popular musical entertainment and a family atmosphere, and helps foster a sense of unity among Jeep owners. "You can't get this type of camaraderie when you buy an Explorer" is the not-so-subtle message.

The Jeep Jamboree USA series of off-road jaunts around the North American continent, plus the multitude of Jeep Exclusive clubs, reinforce the notion that among serious off-roading enthusiasts, Jeeps make up an elite corps.

There's also the matter of affordability. The traditional short wheelbase, soft-top Jeep "Universal" still lives on as the Wrangler, and Chrysler has done a good job of keeping the price of the base Wrangler low. Even so, the world increasingly perceives Jeeps as luxurious sport utility vehicles. Keeping Jeeps accessible to the young people who will thoroughly enjoy them is something Chrysler will be grappling with for years to come. The act of driving a Jeep no longer places the owner's knees up around his ears or his kidneys up around his throat. But the act of purchasing a Jeep does tend to leave bruises on one's wallet.

The traditional soft-top Jeep "Universal" joined the modern world with the introduction of the Wrangler for the 1987 model year. The Wrangler, lower to the ground and wider than its CJ-7 predecessor, was an acknowledgment that more people were using Jeeps for daily transportation, and that safety issues had to be taken more seriously. *Jeep photo*

In addition, government regulation of vehicles will continue. Occasional rumbles from Washington echo with talk of ride-height restrictions or bumper height location.

And a fickle public could change the equation overnight. Will the public want more emphasis on off-road ability, or less? More comfort and convenience, or a lower price? More power or better gas mileage? If Jeep engineers and marketing people were asked, they'd say the public routinely expects all those things.

Recent Jeep concept vehicles such as the Icon and Jeepster V-8 show that the corporation is wrestling with several interpretations of the twen-

ty-first century Jeep. The outlook is positive. The Jeepster looks like a musclecar that's been force-fed bodybuilding workout supplements. And with its 4.7-liter, 32-valve V-8, 19-inch cast-aluminum wheels, and adjustable ride height, that's exactly what it is. The Icon is the ultimate Tonka Toy, the type of vehicle generations of clumsy-fingered children have tried to draw on the backs of their grade-school notebooks.

In other words, they are just the kind of Jeeps that the next generation of children will point to excitedly when they pass by. The future Jeeps, like the first ones, might even produce bedtime stories of their own.

1

DRAFTED FOR DUTY: JEEP'S SPECTACULAR WARTIME PERFORMANCE

The problem, in a nutshell: The military had a hole in its lineup of motorized vehicles. In the 1930s the Army had tanks, trucks, and ambulances, but nothing that could be classified as "light reconnaissance." There was nothing that proved to be a small target for the enemy that could be used to deliver messages to the front lines. There wasn't a vehicle to shuttle small groups of soldiers over rough terrain, or a vehicle that offered speed and maneuverability in combat situations.

The closest vehicle the Army had available for such duties (besides a horse) was a motorcycle with sidecar, which was not exactly the most rugged or flexible platform. Although pickup trucks were used as well, their tall bodywork provided a tempting target on the battlefield. It was this gap in the armed forces motor pool that the Jeep was meant to fill.

The need for such military innovations took on a special urgency during the later Depression years. Although the United States did not enter World War II until the Japanese attack on Pearl Harbor in 1941, the beginnings of global conflict flared up in the mid-1930s. Many officers in the military, not to mention President Franklin Roosevelt and a good number of politicians in the U.S.

The basic shape of the Jeep has not changed much over the years. The square, open body configuration has been a constant for 60 years. From the first Jeeps to the newest examples, the windshield has always folded down.

Early Bantam Scout cars underwent testing at Camp Chaffee, Arkansas. The run of 69 Mark II Jeeps that followed the original test vehicle ditched the original prototype's cycle-style fenders for squared-off units, but can still be identified by their rounded nose and hood. The later "production" Bantams from the first order of 1,500 utilized a squared-off hood. Although the Bantams were the first true Jeeps, they were rarely seen in the United States. Most were shipped overseas to the Soviet Union and Great Britain under the Lend-Lease Act. *U.S. Army Transportation Museum*

"Bantam Rough Riders" are seen testing an early BRC Bantam Jeep. After the original Bantam pilot scout car was put through the wringer at Camp Holabird, the following 69 BRC-60s (shown) were distributed widely among various military outfits for testing. The ability to tow a 37mm anti-tank gun was eventually written right into the Jeep's operations manual, although it's doubtful airborne towing was a requirement. *U.S. Army Transportation Museum*

House and Senate, assumed the United States would eventually be forced to play some part in the various conflicts. The fighting had spread too rapidly to be ignored.

The chain of events that eventually drew the United States into the war started in distant places. In 1936 Germany broke the Locarno Pact of 1925 by occupying the Rhineland. Fighting broke out in Asia, as the Chinese sought to repulse Japanese aggression. On December 13, 1937, Nanking fell to the Japanese, followed by Canton and Hankow in 1938. Germany invaded Austria in 1938, while Italy invaded Albania in 1939. Germany and Italy then formed a military alliance, the core of the Axis union, that year. Both the Germans and the Soviets invaded and promptly conquered Poland in September 1939, dragging Britain and France into the conflict, and officially starting World War II. Denmark, Norway, the Netherlands, Belgium, and Luxembourg fell to the Germans in the spring of 1940.

What Kind of Name Is "Jeep?"

The origins of the Jeep name have always been hard to pin down. One of the earliest known uses of the name comes from 1936, when the "Eugene the Jeep" character debuted in E.C. Segar's *Popeye* comic strip. Soldiers later applied the Jeep tag to Minneapolis-Moline's equipment movers, and other small "general- purpose" military vehicles.

In fact, some maintain the "General- Purpose" acronym, GP, which was applied to the early Jeeps, is the origin of the Jeep name. Saying "GP" fast will get you "Jeep," more or less.

The origin of the Jeep name was just part of the wrangling over the vehicle's past and future. (See Rallying 'Round the Flag sidebar.) But the final determination on the Jeep name worked in Willys-Overland's favor. On June 13, 1950, they were granted the trademark to the Jeep name for commercial use on vehicles.

Meanwhile, the American military of the 1930s was nearly as tattered as the nation's economy. The Great Depression and subsequent tight federal budgets had sapped money from the armed services. Additionally, the horrors of World War I had instilled in Americans a determination to avoid entanglement in future "European Wars." But with a whirlpool of conflict tugging at the United States, the nation needed a rapid upgrade of its military might. The Jeep was part of that effort.

The Jeep, however, was not the first attempt at a light reconnaissance combat vehicle. In 1937 Army Captain Robert G. Howie designed the Howie machine-gun carrier, which met many of the military's requirements. It certainly offered a low battlefield profile, as it was basically nothing more than a rolling chassis and floor pan. A crew of two soldiers operated the Howie carrier and its

machine gun from a prone position. Ultimately, the Howie's light cargo capacity, meager top speed, and room for only two soldiers doomed the project. It did, however, help point the direction for later Jeeps.

The origin of what we recognize as the first Jeep can be traced to 1940. Its development was extensively documented in 1943 by Herbert R. Rifkind in his report for the government, *The Jeep—Its Development and Procurement under the Quartermaster Corps, 1940-1942*. The Rifkind report remains the primary source material on the Jeep's creation.

Detailing the Jeep's genesis was no idle project for Rifkind. The original motivation behind building the Jeep was to produce a simple light reconnaissance vehicle. However, once it was created there was a scramble by nearly everyone involved to take credit, not to mention considerable jockeying among prominent auto companies to secure rights to the Jeep's postwar future. Even the ownership of the "Jeep" name was under dispute. "While the Jeep was probably the most spectacular single accomplishment of the QMC and one of the outstanding successes of any of the supply services of the army in the present war, its conception and birth were not achieved without travail," Rifkind wrote.

There were conflicts within the military over the specifications to which the proposed scout car should conform. The Infantry wanted the vehicle to be light enough for soldiers to lift and carry if necessary. The Quartermaster Corps worried that such demure tonnage would render the Jeep too flimsy for prolonged military abuse. The cowl height was another source of debate, as the new vehicle would have to have a low enough profile to avoid getting easily zapped on the battlefield.

And since there were no available vehicles from the auto industry suitable for such duty, the military would have to set forth the specifications it

The early scout cars from Bantam, Willys, and Ford were not immediately labeled "Jeeps"; the name came later. In fact, on the early 1940s postcard that used this image, the vehicle was referred to as a "U.S. Army Peep." Other names that attached themselves to the Jeep included Blitz Buggy and Mule. *U.S. Army Transportation Museum*

the United States. A 45-ci four-cylinder engine producing 20 horsepower powered the American Austin, which was puny by American standards. The car was substantially smaller than other American cars. It flopped. The company sought bankruptcy protection by 1934 and ceased production by 1936.

American Austin was then sold and renamed the American Bantam Car Company. When production resumed in 1937, Bantam was still a fringe manufacturer of small cars, pickups, and delivery vehicles, and was financially hanging on by its fingernails.

Although an unlikely source for U.S. Army vehicles, there was precedent for working with American Bantam. Austin cars were used successfully in reconnaissance roles in the British military. Earlier in the 1930s, the U.S. Army's Infantry Board requested, and later received, an Austin pickup for evaluation, which showed some promise. And, most significantly, the compact dimensions of the Bantam automobile were in keeping with what the Army had in mind for its new scout car.

As Rifkind reported:

On June 19, 1940, a special subcommittee and Major Howie, whose presence had been requested by the subcommittee so that he could

wanted for its proposed scout car and work closely with automakers to create the final product.

One such automobile company was American Bantam of Butler, Pennsylvania. Founded as American Austin, the company was licensed in 1929 to produce the English Austin compact automobile in

The Ford "Pygmy" prototype, undergoing tests at Holabird Quartermaster Depot. Ford produced 277,896 Jeeps during World War II from plants in Detroit, Michigan; Dallas, Texas; Chester, Pennsylvania; Louisville, Kentucky; and Richmond, California. Jeep production was often a military secret, as was the case at the Dallas Ford facility. Jeeps were loaded onto rail cars inside the factory and shipped to their destinations on the QT. *Ford photo*

After the Quartermaster Corps gave the Willys Quad prototypes the OK, the first run of 1,500 Willys MA Jeeps was put into production in June 1941. The MAs were easily identified by the flattened front edge of their hoods with "Willys" spelled out in block letters. The Willys MA also used a column-mounted shifter. *U.S. Army Transportation Museum*

give full information on his carrier, met with the officials and engineers of the Bantam Company at their Butler, Pennsylvania, plant, for discussion of the possibilities and limitations of the Bantam chassis as a basis for both the proposed command-reconnaissance car and the Howie Weapons Carrier.

The military ran some preliminary tests with the Bantam, which revealed the chassis to be adequate to the task.

For its part, American Bantam was all too happy to work with the Army. By 1940 the company was all but out of business, and creating a successful scout car could lead to government contracts for years to come.

The Blueprints

The Infantry and Cavalry laid out the specifications for the new 1/4-ton vehicle on July 2, 1940.

These specs included four-wheel drive capability with a two-speed transfer case, a maximum wheelbase of 80 inches, an overall height of 40 inches, at least four cylinders underhood, a rectangular body with folding windshield, three bucket seats; a .30 caliber machine gun mount, and an oil bath air cleaner. Weight was to be no more than 1,275 pounds. Performance requirements included approach and departure angles of 45 degrees and 40 degrees, respectively, and an ability to achieve at least 50 miles per hour.

Having specified what it wanted, the Army next solicited bids from the industrial world for the first batch of test vehicles. Thanks in large part to the imposition of the short, September 23 deadline, there was only one other taker besides Bantam—Willys-Overland of Toledo, Ohio. But despite having the low bid, Willys could not come close to meeting the deadline. On July 25, 1940, the contract

One of the two remaining Willys MA Jeeps rests in the collection of the Jeepers Jamboree Museum in California. This rare early model was a Rubicon Trail participant in 1953 and 1954, much to the delight of the regulars. The Jeepers Jamboree purchased the vehicle and had it restored in 1977. It still carries bullet wounds from battle.

hanging over the group and the company's survival at stake, the crew worked virtually nonstop through the late summer.

Their creation, the first Bantam general-purpose scout car, the first real "Jeep," was designed by Karl K. Probst. Probst was hired as Bantam's chief engineer for the scout car project. He worked arm-in-arm with Bantam president Frank Fenn, and factory manager Harold Crist and his team. Although the Army specifications were quite clear, Bantam had to make do with what few resources it had available. Consequently, much of the prototype was handmade, but some of the bodywork was cobbled together from Bantam car parts. The proportions were much the same as later Jeeps, but the prototype employed rounded, cycle-style front fenders. Minor parts such as the dash instruments came directly from a Bantam car.

The prototype was powered by a 45-horsepower, 112-ci four-cylinder engine supplied by Continental Motors Corporation, as the Bantam car engine had been judged too weak. The prototype used a three-speed transmission, a Spicer two-speed transfer case, and Spicer axles. It measured 126 inches long overall and rode on a 79.5-inch wheelbase. Wheels measured 16 inches in diameter.

After the marathon development period, Bantam employees conducted the first prototype test drive on September 21, 1940. The vehicle performed as expected, but there was little time for further testing by the company. The prototype was driven to Camp Holabird on September 23, just barely beating the military's deadline.

At Holabird, the prototype Jeep was, naturally, thrashed to within an inch of its young life. It was driven up all manner of grades, through jungle-quality mud bogs and over the roughest terrain the Army could create. The testers did manage to eventually break the prototype, but not before pronouncing the vehicle fit for duty.

The most difficult specification for Bantam to achieve turned out to be the maximum weight of the vehicle, which had been set by the Army at an unrealistic 1,275 pounds. The prototype weighed 2,030 pounds. "During the construction of the original model, the bugaboo of weight cropped up again," Rifkind reported. "It became evident to both American Bantam and Holabird that strength and material limitations, as well as other engineering factors, would make it virtually impossible to meet the 1,275-pound weight requirement."

for the prototype and first 69 test vehicles went to American Bantam. The short-term prize for Bantam was the contract for 70 vehicles, which were to be used for testing and evaluation by the various branches of the military. The long-term goal, of course, was government contracts for tens of thousands of vehicles.

Working with the Holabird Quartermaster Depot in Baltimore, ground zero for military vehicle torture testing, Bantam engineers started work on a prototype model. With the Army's firm deadline

During World War II Jeeps were rarely seen without their accompanying trailers. The trailers were rated at 1/4 ton, and had a maximum payload of 500 pounds. Overall gross weight of the trailer was 1,050 pounds.

Eventually, the weight limitations were ratcheted up to 2,100 pounds, and later during World War II to 2,450 pounds.

With the lessons learned at Holabird, Bantam made several changes to the following 69 test vehicles, which were labeled BRC-60 Mark IIs. The mechanicals were beefed up. The rounded front fenders were jettisoned for squared-off parts. Eight of the 70 Bantams were equipped with four-wheel steering, a setup the Army was eager to test. (Four-wheel steering was later deemed impractical, as the extra parts, weight, and potential for breakage outweighed the benefits.)

New Competitors

While American Bantam set about building the first batch of 70 Jeeps, competitors started turning hungry eyes toward the potential business. Willys-Overland's bid for the first 70 vehicles had been unsuccessful, but it had certainly not given up on the project. And the Army was openly courting Ford Motor Company, with its vast production capacity.

Many in the military, particularly advocates within the Infantry, thought American Bantam should reap the rewards of its pioneering work on the scout car and be awarded the upcoming larger contracts. They correctly noted that Bantam had cooperated with the government to an unprecedented degree in designing a vehicle on short notice, using virtually all its resources, to the military's specifications. Others disagreed. Many wondered if American Bantam had the capacity to build the scout car in large enough numbers. They believed using multiple suppliers, as was common military policy, would result in a better final product and insulate the program from failure should any one corporation go under.

And American Bantam *was* on shaky ground. By the time the first Jeep was being tested at Holabird, it represented practically the entirety of Bantam's business. For that matter, Willys too had been in financial trouble, although Willys was still considerably larger than Bantam. As Rifkind noted in his 1943 Quartermaster report, "The R.F.C. [Reconstruction Finance Corporation] had come to the rescue of both these concerns, and it was the government's money that enabled them to finance their Jeep contracts. Needless to say, this was not true of Ford."

Just as the Willys MA Jeeps sported "WILLYS" script across the front of the hood, Ford stamped its first Jeeps with its corporate logo across the rear panel, as shown on this early 1942 model. The Army later ordered all such visible corporate identifiers off the Jeeps.

Willys-Overland Go-Devil Engine Specifications

Type	L-head, inline four-cylinder
Displacement	134.2 ci (2,199 cc)
Bore x Stroke	3.125x4.375 inches
Compression ratio	6.48:1
Horsepower	60 @ 4,000 rpm
Torque	105 foot-pounds at 2,000 rpm

If Willys and Ford were to get into the Jeep business, however, they had to produce pilot models for testing. Willys delivered its two "Quad" pilot models to Holabird on November 13, 1940. Ford followed with its "Pygmy" on November 23.

Both vehicles had their own strengths and weaknesses. The Willys Quad was much too heavy, far exceeding the Army's weight limit, but had by far the most powerful engine of the three prototypes. The "Go-Devil" four-cylinder, developed by Delmar "Barney" Roos, chief engineer at Willys, was rated at 60 horsepower. The appearance of the Quad featured a rounded hood with a curved formation of grille bars.

Ford's Pygmy used a modified Ford/Ferguson "Dearborn" tractor engine with a Model A gearbox, not the most awe-inspiring powertrain of the group. But the Ford incorporated unusual yet useful features, such as "swing up" headlamps mounted on a hinged bracket. An advantage of this arrangement was that the headlamps could illuminate the engine compartment. The Ford was also judged to have the most comfortable driving position of the three.

The debate within the Army over which company should be issued the next contracts intensified. The Infantry, eager to expedite Jeep production, believed the contract for the next 1,500 Jeeps should be given to Bantam. The Quartermaster Corps preferred multiple sources. The plan that was nearly adopted consisted of ordering 1,500 Jeeps total, 500 each from American Bantam, Willys-Overland, and Ford. In the fall, the Army reached a compromise that resulted in contracts issued for 4,500 Jeeps, with 1,500 coming from each automaker, pending approval of the Willys and Ford prototypes.

The prototypes were, of course, approved, and suddenly Jeep production was a three-way war in its own right.

Since the Jeep was expected to fight in every climate on earth from Scandanavia to Libya, Jeeps were fitted with all manner of gear to get the job done. The rifle holder pictured allowed quick access to the bulky weapon.

Both Willys-Overland and American Bantam manufactured Jeep 1/4-ton trailers. The trailers, like the 1943 Willys GPT shown, used a simple locking ring-type hitch that made for extremely quick hook-ups. But the trailers were a poor consolation prize for American Bantam, which had hoped to win large government contracts as a reward for its pioneering work on the Jeep.

Rallying 'Round the Flag

Although it has not always been the case throughout American history, patriotism was a valuable marketing concept during World War II. Most American industrial concerns trumpeted their contributions to the war effort in dramatic full-page advertisements in the popular magazines of the day. Certainly much of this was heartfelt and genuine pride in helping defend the nation, but the advertising blitz also served an old-fashioned commercial purpose. By jumping into the foxhole with American GIs, as it were, corporations hoped the public would remember them when it came time to buy a new battery, or tires, or piston rings, or maybe even someday a new car.

Willys-Overland was as patriotic as any other automaker, but it had an ulterior motive for its flag-waving advertising campaign. Due to the success of the Jeep on the battlefield (and in the hearts and minds of the American people), there was a considerable struggle for the rights to the name "Jeep." Throughout the war years "Jeep" was a generic name applied to all the small 1/4-ton four-wheel-drive reconnaissance vehicles built by Willys, American Bantam, and Ford. The name trickled up from the foxholes and encampments of the military, rather than descending from some lofty corporate boardroom.

Securing the name for its own products would be a tremendous coup for any automaker. The goodwill the Jeep had accumulated during the war would benefit any company able to use the name. After all, there were postwar sales to consider.

The battle that waged in the corporate boardrooms was nearly as fierce as the real war. Besides the Army itself, several companies had a hand in the creation and production of the Jeep. American Bantam built the first running prototype, but Willys and Ford built Jeeps in large numbers. Additionally, Minneapolis-Moline Power Implement Company had converted farm tractors into 4x4 artillery movers, which were sometimes called "Jeeps" by National Guardsman who had been testing the vehicles at Camp Ripley. Minneapolis-Moline tried vigorously, and ultimately unsuccessfully, to claim the name for itself in national advertising.

In order to help establish Jeep as its own trademark (the company filed a trademark application in February 1943), Willys-Overland commissioned a series of advertisements highlighting the company's prominent role in the Jeep's life. These ads later proved to be some of the most memorable print advertisements of the century. The ads featured realistic paintings of actual battle scenes and real-life portrayals of military life, rendered by a series of accomplished artists.

James Sessions (1882-1962) was one such artist. Sessions studied at the Art Institute of Chicago, and worked as an illustrator with various studios in Chicago. During World War II he also worked for the Navy, painting battle scenes. Sessions produced dozens of watercolors for Willys-Overland's Jeep campaign, with such gutsy titles as "Givin' 'em Hell at Guadalcanal," and "Signal Corps Unit Beats Ring of Death."

Advertisements like this 1943 example memorializing the 5th Army's landing at Salerno, illustrated by James Sessions, show how Willys sought to both display the company's patriotism and link the Jeep to the Willys-Overland company. The strength of the Go-Devil engine was a main selling point.

The illustrations were accompanied by hard-hitting text, some of which read as if the words were ripped from the notes of some fevered war correspondent. In the ad "A Bellyful of Hell for Hitler," the text read:

Yes sir!—a bellyful of misery and hell—the kind that American and British fighting men in North Africa—and Russian fighting men from Moscow to the Caucasus, mounted in tough Jeeps built by Willys-Overland, are dealing out to a badly addled Hitler and his deluded gang.

Some of the ads were almost poetic. In the "Vive Les Americains! Vive La France! Vive Le Jeep!" ad from late 1944, the text reads:

On the morning of August 17th, 1944, Nazi-infested Orleans came suddenly alive. The air was charged with suppressed excitement. Emotions were masked, but French hearts beat wildly. For the glorious news was being flashed from lip to ear, that the victorious Americans were marching toward the city. Liberation was at hand.

All that day and night the air trembled from the violence of the fighting. Next morning a joyful, almost hysterical Orleans realized that the hated Nazis had fled.

Other notable illustrators employed in Willys-Overland's Jeep campaign included Benton Clark and John Langley Howard. Most of Howard's scenes were set away from the battlefield, with more fanciful images picturing Willys' "Go-Devil" engine towing farm implements around the globe, or some such similar situation.

Ford Motor Company also produced advertisements featuring the company's Jeeps. And many manufacturers of individual Jeep components incorporated the vehicle into their patriotic advertising as well.

But Willys-Overland took the use of the Jeep name further than any other company, eventually experiencing the wrath of the Federal Trade Commission. Responding to objections from other manufacturers, the FTC issued a complaint on May 6, 1943.

The gist of the complaint was that Willys claimed to help in the creation of the Jeep when in fact it had not, and that its Jeep was the pattern for all other Jeeps, a half-truth at best. Further, Willys wasn't the sole manufacturer of the Jeep, and linking Jeeps to Willys-Overland passenger cars in advertisements was

Willys-Overland wasn't the only corporation that cashed in on the Jeep's wartime success. Permite Replacement Parts, maker of the Jeep's pistons, valves, and water pump shaft, was eager to tout its contributions to the project.

a dubious assertion. The company was ordered to cease and desist any claims that it "created or designed" the Jeep.

But in the end Willys-Overland came out the big winner, mainly because it had been the only company to continually produce Jeeps after the war. Also, American Bantam closed its doors, Minneapolis-Moline's complaints were dismissed, and Ford had its hands full revamping its entire car and truck lineup for the postwar market. As one of its more blatant ads from 1944 stated, Willys and Jeep had indeed become "Linked together in the minds of millions." A trademark to the Jeep name was granted Willys-Overland in June 1950.

Very early production Jeeps like the Willys MA used a single bow for the canvas top, while later models, such as this 1942 Ford GPW, used two bows for the top. The gas tank and filler were located under the driver seat.

interchangeability of parts, maximum speed of production, and large production capacity. Despite its strenuous objections, Bantam was dropped from the Jeep program in late 1941. The company's small size, which had helped it respond so quickly in the production of the original Jeep pilot model, crippled the company when it came time for large-scale production.

As Rifkind noted in 1943:

First, Bantam was never able to demonstrate to the Quartermaster Corps' satisfaction, as Ford had done, a plan for the production of the standardized Willys model that would provide additional sources for production of bottleneck items without further strain on the already critical machine tool industry. The new and separate set of facilities provided by Ford for producing axle and joint bottleneck items for the Jeep, tooled entirely by itself, meant that the entire output of Spicer on these items could now flow to the Willys assembly line.

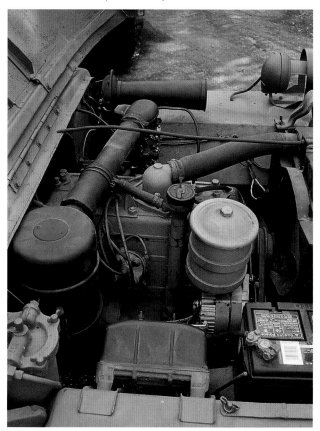

The Go-Devil engine was the deciding factor in the selection of the Willys as the template for the standardized Jeep model. The Willys-spec Ford GPWs, like this 1942 model, still had many parts stamped with the stylized Ford "F." The alternator shown on this example is a later addition.

bringing 20.9 miles per gallon. The powerful Willys came in last at 20.2 miles per gallon. The Ford GP had the shortest turning radius, but the weakest brakes. All were judged acceptable in cross-country trials.

As a result of these tests, the Infantry Board was able to make recommendations for future standardized models. Their conclusion, as reported in Rifkind's report, was that "the standard vehicle should be based upon the Willys chassis, with the Ford shift lever and handbrake arrangement, and performance characteristics of the Willys."

Besides the fact that Willys won the performance duel (and soon after a contract for 18,600 Jeeps, after turning in the lowest bid), changes in the Army's procurement policy in early July hurt Bantam further. The new policy put emphasis on

The simple canvas top was not much protection from the elements, and the overall comfort level caused no loss of sleep at the Cadillac offices. Yet the Jeep still earned remarkable affection from American soldiers. The Jeep was a fixture in Bill Mauldin's Willie and Joe cartoons in *Stars and Stripes*, helping establish the Jeep's reputation as a faithful comrade in arms. *U.S. Army Transportation Museum*

Further, ". . . by 1942 it was plainly evident that the combined productive capacity of Willys and Ford was going to be more than sufficient to handle all future Army and lend-lease requirements for the Jeep."

Bantam's freeze-out from future Jeep contracts didn't pass unnoticed. The Truman Committee, headed by future president Harry S. Truman, had been initiated in the Senate in August 1941 with the task of investigating defense appropriations. Specifically, the committee was concerned about the treatment of small businesses in the appropriation process. The Jeep contract wars attracted the Senate committee's notice, along with that of the House Military Affairs Committee. Bantam also appealed to Senator Joseph S. Guffey of Pennsylvania for assistance.

In the end, however, larger events overshadowed Bantam's arguments. Once the Japanese bombed Pearl Harbor in December 1941, yanking the United States from the sidelines of World War II and into the leading role, reliable, volume production became the standard by which defense contractors were judged. Appropriations policies that favored small businesses were often overlooked in favor of larger suppliers. Bantam was

given a handful of small contracts for two-wheel trailers to be used with the Jeep, but the company never again produced Jeeps for the military. As with smaller nations in the real war, the tiny American Bantam Corporation stood no chance of winning its own marketplace skirmishes against the larger automotive titans.

One Jeep, Two Makers

From 1942 until the end of the war, Willys and Ford were the sole builders of Jeeps. The Willys standardized model—Willys MB in that company's nomenclature, Ford GPW over at Blue Oval headquarters—was produced in staggering numbers, and sent on assignment worldwide. Appearance-wise, the first Willys MBs looked more like the original Ford and Bantam Jeeps than Willys' own MA model, at least from the front. The early MBs, also known as "slat grille" MBs, utilized the thin prison bar grille appearance common to the early Fords.

The thin grille bars of the MA and early MB gave way to the now-familiar stamped, flat, 8-bar grille face in 1942. Under the skin, however, beat the heart of the Willys Go-Devil engine.

The capabilities and specifications of the Willys standardized model, as culled from War Department technical manuals of the time, included an angle of approach of 45 degrees and angle of departure of 35 degrees. Ground clearance was 8 3/4 inches, while payload was listed at 800 pounds.

After victory in World War II, the Jeep returned home a hero, as this Armistice Day parade in Austin, Texas, 1945, shows. Nearly 650,000 Jeeps were produced during the war. *Austin History Center, Austin Public Library*

Other Branches of the Family Tree

The Jeep was the trailblazer when it came to quarter-ton military transport. Yet that hasn't stopped succeeding generations of engineers from trying to improve upon or update the original. Even as far back as World War II, when the original Jeep was still a newborn, the U.S. military hoped to develop a Jeep light enough to be parachuted from the belly of a bomber, among other functions.

One company that had an early hand in trying to develop an ultralight Jeep was Crosley. Like American Bantam, Crosley specialized in building small delivery vehicles. Although its Jeep proposal never caught on, the company did produce a handful of "Pup" utility vehicles for the Navy.

The need for a Jeep light enough to be lifted by helicopter into battle led to the development of the Mighty Mite 1/4-ton in the 1950s. Designated the M422 by the military (M422A1 in long wheelbase form), the first prototypes were built in 1953. Engineers used every trick in the book to cut weight. The final production version of the Mighty Mite was powered by a 108-ci, air-cooled V-4 (air-cooled engines require no coolant, saving liquid weight) that produced 55 horsepower at 3,600 rpm and 90 foot-pounds of torque at 2,500 rpm. Aluminum body panels were used, and the overall dimensions were smaller than that of the Jeep. The vehicle weighed roughly 1,500 pounds, fairly close to the Army's original weight goal for the first Jeeps. American Motors built the Mighty Mite for the U.S. Marines from 1960 to 1963. Approximately 4,000 were built.

In 1968 *Four-Wheeler* magazine writers took a spin in a Mighty Mite that had been released from military service and sold at auction. The writers found advantages to the Mite's small size and agility. "Taking the 'Mite' for a spin is quite a sensation," they wrote. "As its name implies, its

The Army explored the feasibility of extremely lightweight Jeeps capable of being easily transported and parachuted from aircraft. The Jeep-like vehicle pictured is believed to be a Crosley lightweight. Crosley, another American manufacturer of miniature vehicles, built even smaller cars than Bantam, powered by air-cooled two-cylinder engines. Crosley eventually produced a "Pup" utility vehicle for the Navy. U.S. Army Transportation Museum

performance is quick and seat pinning. Rounding curves is like that of a sports car, no lean or roll-over sensation. Gearing is low and highway speeds up around 55 mph is really pushing the Mite."

Handling proved a handicap for another Jeep replacement, the M151. In appearance, the M151 more closely resembled the original Jeep. In fact, Vietnam-era veterans often refer to it as a Jeep, although the vehicle sprang from a different bloodline and never had a civilian counterpart. The M151 was built by Ford (and later, AM General) and utilized the basic proportions of the traditional Jeep, although the horizontally slotted grille is one quick way to distinguish the M151 from Willys and Kaiser Jeeps.

As a vehicle designed for even more specialized military use, the M151 had its share of quirks. Most notable was its four-wheel independent suspension design, which made the M151 prone to rolling over. Although quite capable off-road, on road surfaces the M151 gave little or no warning before going bottom-side-up. The Army even had a special training course for driving the M151. A later edition, the M151 A1, did little to stabilize the vehicle's handling or reputation.

In 1970 an M151 A2 with semi-independent rear suspension with trailing arms was introduced, finally fixing the quarter-ton's handling. Fortunately, few civilians ever experienced the M151's nasty personality, since in 1971 the National Highway Safety Administration and U.S. Department of Transportation recommended against sales of surplus M151s to the public. Only a few worked their way into civilian hands.

Next came what is perhaps the most recognizable military vehicle since the original Jeep, and just in time to replace all those aging M38A1s and M151s. Built by AM General, the High-Mobility Multi-Purpose Wheeled Vehicle (HMMWV) took everything about the Jeep and made it bigger. The "Humvee," as it was nicknamed, had a whopping 16 inches of ground clearance and was 85 inches wide to improve sidehill stability. Four- and six-cylinder powerplants were left behind, as the Humvee was powered by a 6.2-liter diesel V-8 supplied by General Motors. The Humvee was produced in several body styles. Production began in January 1985.

Just as World War II had made the Willys and Ford Jeeps famous worldwide, the Gulf War of 1991 propelled the Humvee into the spotlight. With global television audiences watching the capable Humvee dash about the Iraqi desert for weeks on end, more than a few people decided they'd like one of their own. After the war, AM General federalized the vehicle, now called the Hummer, for retail sale. With its high price tag the Hummer will never fill the same role in the automotive world as the Jeep does, but it has carved out its own high-profile niche. It seems only fitting that a company that once built military Jeeps should create the perfect replacement.

Bendix supplied the hydraulic brakes. The gas tank was located under the driver seat. Tires were knobby 6.00x16 units. A starting crank was provided with all Jeeps.

But modifications during wartime were frequent, as the Jeeps assumed more diverse duties. The charging system was changed from 6 volts to 12 volts later during the war, and improved cooling systems for desert use were incorporated.

In fact, the Jeep blueprint proved so useful that the Army proposed spin-offs. Ford production expanded to include the GPA amphibious Jeep, also called the "Seep." The 1/4-ton Amphibian project was initiated in earnest starting in March 1941. The GPA was expected to approximate, in size and function, the regular land-based Jeep, but attain speeds of approximately 5 miles per hour in the water, with minimal time needed to effect the changeover.

Pilot models were presented on February 18, 1942. Ford and Marmon-Herrington both bid for the contracts, although Ford, once again because of its superior production capacity, handily won. The first pilot Seep weighed about 3,600 pounds, and attained speeds of 7 miles per hour in water.

The specs for the amphibious Jeep read much like those for the land-based version. Designed for a crew of two, although fitted with five life preservers, the Seep had a payload of 800 pounds. Ground clearance was 8 7/8 inches, and tires were 6.00x16 inches. Fuel tank capacity was 15 gallons.

On April 10 or 11 of 1942, General Frink, Chief of the QMC Motor Transport Division, gave Ford the green light for the production of 5,000 amphibious Jeeps, with a rush order attached. These first amphibious Jeeps were produced from September to December 1942. Eventually, 12,778 GPAs were contracted, although not all were built. The execution of the GPA turned out to be less than successful, and the vehicle was not as universally useful as its land-based cousin.

A New Weapon

It would be nearly impossible to list all the uses for the Jeep during World War II. As the amphibious Jeep illustrated, the Jeep was not just used in support and reconnaissance roles, as first intended, but as a weapon as well.

Innovative military leaders were quick to discover the Jeep's potential as an offensive weapon. A fine example of this expanded role was the British

Jeep raid against the German air base at Sidi Haneish in Egypt, near the Mediterranean coast, on July 26, 1942. The British Long Range Desert Group conceived an attack plan using the Jeeps as a quick strike force. They believed the Jeeps were the ideal weapons with which to strike the air base at night, when the German warplanes were on the ground.

The 18-Jeep group was led that night by Captain David Sterling. A driver and two gunners manned each of the Jeeps, with guns equipped with incendiary and tracer ammunition. During the attack, the two columns of Jeeps fanned out into a V-formation, firing into the rows of grounded aircraft. The group moved quickly along the edge of the airfield, inflicting as much damage as possible before fleeing back into the desert.

The rapid attack caught the Germans unaware. Sterling and his men destroyed 25 Stuka dive bombers, Junkers 52s, and Heinkels, and damaged several other aircraft. Afterward, the Jeep raiders scattered into the desert, traveling as far as they could in the remaining darkness, and then holing up during the daylight hours, camouflaging themselves as best they could.

What Sterling's raid illustrated was the offensive potential of a small, fast, maneuverable, four-wheel-drive vehicle like the Jeep. Though lightly armored, the Jeep could travel places that larger, more cumbersome vehicles could not, and do so with greater stealth.

New Generations

As World War II drew to its conclusion in 1945, military Jeep production ended. With the Axis powers defeated there was hardly need for more than half a million Jeeps in the military motor pool. So after the war, thousands of Jeeps were sold for scrap metal, or as surplus vehicles, or were simply pushed over the edge of aircraft carrier decks. Many others were left in the foreign countries to which they had been assigned, for use by the locals.

But war was never far away in the mid-twentieth century world, and military Jeep production was revived for the Korean War (1950–1953). The first of the new generation of military Jeeps was designated the M38 and was built in 1950 and 1951. The M38 was a militarized version of the CJ-3A, which had replaced the CJ-2A in the Willys-Overland postwar civilian lineup. In regards to

War-era Ford GPWs were fitted with "entrenching tools" and axes along the body sides. Though still small, the Jeep was considerably more capable and practical than a motorcycle with sidecar, which had been the reconnaissance vehicle of the 1930s.

The M38 Willys Jeep, built in 1950 and 1951, earned its stripes and accolades in the Korean War. It was also a Cold War fixture. The M38 pictured is carrying inspectors to the Yucca Flats nuclear test site in April 1955, prior to Operation Cue. *Camp Mabry Military Museum*

appearance, a one-piece windshield replaced the older-style two-piece windshield, and conventional windshield wipers were mounted below the windshield. Larger headlamps changed the Jeep's face somewhat, although the family resemblance to the World War II Jeeps was unmistakable. Mechanically, the M38 was upgraded with a stout Spicer 44 rear axle. Willys produced 60,345 M38s.

The M38's life was short, however. Later in 1951 the baton was passed to the M38A1, which became the basis for the civilian CJ-5 in 1954. While the M38 was more an extension of the original Jeep MB, the M38A1 represented the next generation of Jeeps. The rounded bodywork was a departure from the folded and squared appearance of the first Jeeps. The M38A1 rode on a 1-inch

longer wheelbase than the M38, and was 6 inches longer in overall length. The body was wider and roomier. The M38A1 was heavier, at 2,740 pounds, but with its larger gas tank had a longer cruising range, up to 280 miles.

More significant, the A1 arrived with the F-head four-cylinder engine (see chapter 3) underhood, which offered 72 horsepower, a large boost over the L-head's 60 horsepower. The F-head was sparked by a 24-volt ignition system with dual batteries. Between 1951 and 1963, there were 90,529 M38A1s built. Eventually, after a long life, the M38A1s were replaced by similar vehicles from other manufacturers, such as the M151 and, later, the Hummer.

How did the later military Jeeps perform under the lash? Chief Warrant Officer CW3 (ret.)

James Butcher, an MP in the Army, served during the Korean War in the 24th Division. He entered the Army in March 1951, left in February 1954, and reentered in November 1958, staying in until his retirement in January 1976. As an MP, Butcher got the opportunity to drive every type of Jeep made. In fact, like many soldiers from that era who grew up in big cities, he learned how to drive in a Jeep. "It was not unusual for me to enter the Army in 1951, at the age of 18, and not know how to drive," he recalled. At first, when he served in the infantry, a lack of driving skill was no big deal; but after moving to the military police, it was a *very* big deal.

Fortunately, learning to drive a Jeep proved easy. "In the Jeeps from World War II, they were so worn out you could sit there without using the clutch pedal and run the gears," he said. "It was so easy to drive I really enjoyed it."

Butcher recalled that making do with yesterday's equipment was standard operating procedure. "At the end of World War II, there were a lot of vehicles left over that wound up being dumped in the Pacific and Atlantic oceans," he said, which created shortages when Korea came around. "In the Far East, they set up an ordnance depot in Japan where they rebuilt vehicles—Jeeps, trucks, tanks, what have you—we kept reusing them because at the end of World War II we had thrown everything away, and the Congress of the United States was tight; there was no money. So rather than buy new, we used the old."

The military relied on a variety of Jeep vehicles through the years, not just the scout cars. Shown is an ambulance made from a Willys station wagon during field exercises of Operation Cue, a nuclear weapon test. The wreckage in the foreground is the remains of the two-story brick house, shown in the previous photo, 4,700 feet from the blast. *Camp Mabry Military Museum*

Production of the M38A1 Jeep began in 1951; the civilian version, the CJ-5, commenced in 1954. Although still rough around the edges, the M38A1 offered more room and a more comfortable driving environment than the World War II–era Jeeps. M38A1 equipment included a 24-volt electrical system. The hood cutout was for high-water snorkel equipment, which kept water from flooding the engine.

Although fondly remembered by most soldiers, the World War II–vintage Jeeps were certainly no Cadillacs. "The World War II variety Jeeps had a pad for a [seat] cushion. So everybody wound up getting hemorrhoids," Butcher said. "There was no cushioning." Many soldiers worked their own magic to make the Jeeps a bit more comfortable. "We didn't have doors on them," Butcher recalled. " So we had our Japanese carpenters build plywood doors. They had a little frame on a window that slid up and down. We were in northern Japan, and it gets very cold up there."

According to Butcher, not all Jeeps were created—or treated—equal. He remembers when the M38A1s were new and they were used mostly in noncombat units, while the MBs were still used in the fighting divisions. The World War II-era MBs were very reliable, he said, but the M38A1 was much more comfortable. "I had fewer problems in those [the MB] than I did the other ones," he said. "I think the way the mechanics seemed to fix them, they seemed to do it faster and easier on the old Jeep [MB] than they could the new [M38A1]."

Butcher was stationed in Germany in 1959. His unit had the M38, which he recalled as his least favorite. "You couldn't keep them ready for inspection," he remembered. "If you drove the thing a block, it loosened everything up. You could not keep them tight. The prop shafts were always a problem."

Even with a vehicle as simple as the Jeep, the issue of one-upmanship arose. "The company commander and Provost Marshall of the division, their vehicles, they were in top shape all the time," Butcher said. "They had a better paint job. They used to throw a little black in the paint so that everybody else would have the dull ODs. We had ours a little shinier."

As can be imagined in the case of war-ravaged nations, Jeep theft was common in Japan, Korea, and the Philippines, not to mention military shenanigans between different branches of the service. "Everything on *McHale's Navy* was not a lie," Butcher said. Overall, though, Butcher held the Jeep in the same high regard as the countless legions of soldiers around the world. "The Jeep was with us all the time. It's a great, great vehicle."

2

RECREATION BOOM:
THE POSTWAR YEARS

The Jeep returned home a war hero. Needless to say, Willys-Overland was not shy about lifting this particular soldier onto its corporate shoulders for the traditional hero's welcome. Postwar ad campaigns heavily emphasized the Jeep's role in the war effort while at the same time stressing the vehicle's do-anything nature. In fact, the ads often featured several illustrations on the same page showing Jeeps earning their keep at the power plant, or gas station, or duck blind. Willys threw images of every kind of function for the Jeep it could think of at the general public. *Something* was bound to stick.

An ad from late 1945 shouted, "The 'Universal Jeep.' Use it as a truck . . . Use it as a tractor . . . Use it as a runabout . . . Use it as a mobile power unit." To hear Willys tell it, the Jeep wasn't just four-wheeled transportation. "The Universal 'Jeep,' designed for peace, will write a history of its own—the record of a new-day vehicle that will help people around the world do their work easily, swiftly and at low cost," the advertisement promised.

Certainly one of the most unique Jeep profiles belonged to the CJ-3B, with its raised hood. But the high hoodline was for a good cause, it housed a more powerful F-head four-cylinder engine. The CJ-3B went into production for the 1953 model year (shown), and stayed in production alongside the CJ-5 until 1968. During that time span, 155,494 were built in the United States; even more were assembled overseas.

Willys was eager to suggest ways the Jeep might find a place in the postwar world and, as this 1945 ad illustrated by James Sessions shows, it wasn't waiting for the war to end to start the sales pitch. The old 1/4-ton Army mule Jeeps and the postwar Jeeps that followed are the direct progenitors of today's sport utilities. Other manufacturers had pickups and panel trucks, but nothing quite like the Jeep Universal. And today's modern sport ute looks a lot like the Jeep all-steel station wagon introduced in 1946.

In 1946 ad campaigns promoted the Jeep as "World-famous for Power and Usefulness." The ads went on to describe, "Willys-Overland's 4-in-1 Jeep . . . On every continent, the familiar front of the 'Jeep' is a symbol of power out of proportion to size . . . of unique ability to 'do almost anything'—and keep on doing it."

Heck, the Jeep was a product with global reach and lofty intentions, according to Charles E. Sorensen, president of Willys in the immediate postwar period. In a *Saturday Evening Post* ad from

1946, he gave us a glimpse of that vision: "Here at Willys-Overland, we see our Universal 'Jeep' not as another motor vehicle, but as a new means of applying motive power to the world's work," he wrote. "We believe that the 'Jeep' brings the world a new tool with which man can do his work faster, easier, and more economically."

In fact, the brainy engineers at Willys-Overland weren't the only ones who studied far-flung alternate uses for the Jeep. The U.S. Department of Agriculture conducted tests of possible uses for the Jeep at its Farm Tillage Laboratory in Auburn, Alabama, from April 13 to 15, 1942. As Herbert Rifkind reported for the Office of the Quartermaster General in 1943:

> The field tests in which they were tried included pulling practically every kind of implement used in operations necessary to the raising of a crop. Without faltering, the Jeeps plowed the field, prepared the seed bed with double disk and tooth harrows, seeded with a grain drill and two-row cotton or corn planter, and harvested a crop of rye with a mowing machine.

In the government's view, keeping the Jeep down on the farm would be its best postwar use. "Of all the possible peacetime uses to which the Jeep type of vehicle might be put after the war, probably the most important commercial application will be in the field of agriculture," Rifkind concluded. Naturally, the government was wrong.

Time to Sell

Considering Willys-Overland's market position in the postwar world, it's no surprise the company pushed the Jeep as its superstar. Immediately prior to World War II, Willys' model lineup consisted of the four-cylinder Americar, a pickup truck, and a panel delivery van. The four-cylinder engine, which was a rarity among American cars, gave the Willys a distinct position in the market. Yet the Willys corporation was a gnat compared to General Motors, Ford, Chrysler, even Studebaker. Total Willys calendar year production for 1940 was a mere 32,930 vehicles. Ford produced 599,175 cars for calendar year 1940.

Relatively small as it was, Willys did not have adequate resources to go toe-to-toe with the industry giants of the day—especially with the tidal wave of new models soon to debut. With virtually all automotive production devoted to the war effort, there was huge pent-up demand for new cars among the general populace. But the Jeep was still new and had no direct competitors in the market. Plus, the Jeep could be counted on to generate future government contracts and respectable international sales. Consequently, a postwar Americar never materialized. Willys eventually introduced its line of Aero sedans for 1952. But in the immediate postwar period it was the sale of Jeeps that kept the light bill paid at Willys-Overland headquarters. New models that were given priority consisted of variations on the Jeep theme, such as pickup trucks and station wagons.

Observers considered this strategy no sure thing. *Fortune* magazine, in an August 1946 profile of Willys, noted:

The Jeep is a unique vehicle that deserves a longer life than it probably will enjoy. As a fad it is selling even in passenger-car markets now, though by such standards it is uncomfortable and expensive. Generically, it is a piece of machinery and has to be sold as such. In the long run, Willys' Jeep sales (except for export) will depend largely on the ability of its dealers to develop the techniques that sell tractors and machinery. Unless automobile salesmen have changed a lot, the Jeep is a worthy piece of business that may pass away by default.

Willys called the civilian Jeeps "Universals," although the official model designation was CJ. The first Universals were actually released before the end of the war, in 1944 and 1945. These CJ-2

The 1946 Willys station wagon was the company's second attempt to market a civilian Jeep vehicle, after the CJ-2A. At first the station wagon was only sold in two-wheel-drive form, but a four-wheel-drive option was added in 1949. The wagon was also available in a sedan delivery model. *Jeep photo.*

The consumer market Jeeps, like this 1946 CJ-2A, were civilized with such extravagances as a side-mounted spare tire, a tailgate, a windshield wiper, a side-mounted fuel filler neck, and a color selection. An upgraded Borg Warner T-90 transmission, improved rear axle, and more "streetable" gears made the Jeep easier to live with. Since the ownership to the Jeep name was still in dispute, the immediate postwar CJ-2A Jeeps had only "Willys" identifiers stamped into the side of the hood, tailgate, and base of the windshield. *Jeep photo*

"AgriJeeps" were produced to test agricultural uses for the Jeep. In 1944 12 were produced, followed by slightly less than two dozen in 1945.

A model for more general consumption, the CJ-2A, also went into production in 1945. The CJ-2A differed from its conscripted cousins in that it came standard with a side-mounted spare tire, a rear tailgate in place of the MB's solid rear panel, larger headlamps, and actual colors inspired by the rainbow, rather than the Quartermaster Corps. The fuel filler neck for the 10 1/2-gallon gas tank was moved from under the driver's seat to the side of the vehicle. Willys claimed the Universal had an 800-pound capacity in its "bed," with the rear seat removed, and a 5,500-pound towing capacity. The top speed was listed at 60 miles per hour.

All Jeep Universals had four-wheel drive and revised gear ratios better suited for street use. Hardware upgrades included a Spicer 41 rear axle, and a

Borg-Warner three-speed transmission, which replaced the more troublesome GPW T-84 tranny.

Options were few, but useful, such as a power take-off, listed for $96.25, a pulley drive, a front canvas top, a metal top, and special wheels with 7.00-inch tires. The immediate postwar Universals were priced between $1,100 and $1,200. A total of 1,824 Universals were produced for 1945. Willys-Overland built 71,455 Universal Jeeps for 1946, plus assorted station wagons. The company topped that figure in 1947 with the production of 77,958 Universals.

These were good figures considering the average Willys-Overland dealership also had to compete against the large number of surplus military Jeeps entering the postwar market. A few surplus Jeeps even trickled out into the public's hands before the end of the war. *Life* magazine reported in January 1944 on the first few dozen Jeeps released

Discover how useful a car can be

'Jeep' Station Wagon

NO WONDER 'Jeep' Station Wagon owners marvel at their gas mileage! At speeds above 30, an overdrive cuts engine speed 30%, traveling you 42% farther for every turn of the engine.

WITH SEATS REMOVED, you have 98 cubic feet of load space, more with the tailgate lowered. Seats and interior are washable. It's a truly useful car, with double utility for greater value.

Talk to 'Jeep' Station Wagon owners to discover how useful a car can be—how economical and all-around satisfying.

They'll tell you it's grand for families—a comfortable passenger car, with upholstery children won't harm . . . and, with seats out, a practical vehicle for hauling, too.

Women will tell you how easily it handles, how smoothly it rides on rough roads. Men will brag on mileage and low maintenance.

See it now at Willys-Overland dealers— the *first* station wagon with an all-steel body.

THE NEW *'Jeep' Station Sedan* is an entirely new type of car . . . giving you the spaciousness of a station wagon and the luxurious comfort of a sedan. There is unusual leg and head room for six in its all-steel body, plus a large, accessible luggage space. Its new Willys-Overland '6' Engine, with overdrive, gives smooth performance, together with remarkable gasoline mileage. You'll like everything about it, including its smart styling.

WILLYS-OVERLAND MOTORS, TOLEDO • MAKERS OF AMERICA'S MOST USEFUL VEHICLES

The station wagon was the first of the postwar vehicles to take its place beside the civilian Universal. Despite being the first station wagon with an all-steel body, a selling point in advertisements, the paint scheme was intended to simulate wood paneling, a popular feature on many station wagons of the 1940s. Ads like this one from 1948 emphasized the wagon's thriftiness, thanks to the overdrive transmission. *Jeep photo*

With high ground clearance, four-wheel drive, a short turning radius, and an economical four-cylinder engine, the postwar civilian Jeeps were useful in all kinds of environments. *Texas Department of Transportation*

into civilian ownership. "Since the Jeep made its Army debut three years ago the motor-minded American public has coveted it with an unholy covetousness." The article went on to say "To acquire one is the postwar dream of millions of civilians. Last week that dream unexpectedly came true for a handful of lucky Midwestern families." *Life* reported the Heines family of Lucas, Kansas, were "possibly the first civilian Jeep owners in the U.S." It also reported 27 of the first group were shipped to Texas.

The Universal gave Willys-Overland strong sales and a unique position in the market, but a one-car showroom was a risky business strategy. The postwar expansion beyond the Universal was led by Willys president Sorensen, engineer Barney Roos, and designer Brooks Stevens. Using a recognizable Jeep face as a styling foundation on which to build, Stevens penned a completely new lineup of Jeep products to complement the Universal. The first such vehicle was the Jeep station wagon, released in 1946.

The form for most of the new postwar Jeeps was largely dictated by the financial fortunes of Willys-Overland. Stevens' hands were tied in the design of the station wagon, as few suppliers were willing to shove aside profitable (and promptly paid) work from General Motors or Ford in order to stamp sheet metal for the historically shaky Willys-Overland. Sheet-metal suppliers were eventually rounded up, but not the usual ones. The station wagon's body parts were stamped at a home appliance plant, and were subject to the limitations of the factory's equipment. In other words, Jeep's new wagon would not be clothed in the swooping fenders and dramatic curves of other new cars. The wagon's sharply folded refrigerator silhouette was a necessity.

But the Jeep station wagon did blaze a few new trails. It was the first all-steel American station wagon, even if the body contours and paint simulated the expensive wood finish traditionally seen on station wagons. Initially the station wagon was available as a seven-window model, but a panel wagon joined the lineup in 1947.

Postwar Jeeps weren't just used as farm implements or hunting vehicles. With a little custom bodywork they made great tour vehicles in the Rocky Mountains. To this day, Jeep tour companies operate in the Colorado Mountains. *Noble Post Cards*

The FC-series Forward Control pickups were another addition to the growing Jeep line in the 1950s. With a cab over engine layout, four-wheel drive, and low-cut cargo bed, the FC-series trucks made a nice platform for fitting seats appropriate for tour groups. *Noble Post Cards*

The CJ-3B's tall hoodline was created to accommodate the F-head 134-ci four-cylinder. The engine, with its taller cylinder head (which housed the intake valves; the exhaust valves remained in the block), did not fit under the lower CJ-3A hood.

Fortune magazine cut to the heart of the matter in its 1946 review of upcoming Jeep products:

> With its jaunty Jeep bonnet, square fenders, and sleek body, the Willys wagon is a fetching piece. But the significance lies in the attempt it represents to mass-produce what has heretofore been a luxury vehicle [as station wagons were considered at the time].

Sheet-metal limitations aside, the Jeep station wagon was, at least, a mostly new and unique vehicle. It did not share its chassis with the CJ-2A, and

rode on a 104-inch wheelbase. The station wagon was available with two-wheel drive initially, but four-wheel drive was made available for 1949. The wagon also had an independent front suspension. One feature it did share with the Universal, however, was its 63-horsepower four-cylinder powerplant—not much engine for a vehicle of the wagon's bulk.

As production cranked up, 6,534 wagons were built for 1946, followed by 27,515 for 1947. As with the Universal, however, Willys-Overland saw great opportunities for the station wagon in foreign markets. Its rugged construction, ease of maintenance, and relative low cost made the wagon ideal for countries where wages were lower and paved infrastructure less developed. Wagons and Universals were built and sold from Japan to Mexico to Europe, but one of the largest markets was South America. *Willys do Brazil* produced restyled versions of the station wagon, named the "Rural Willys," for sale throughout the continent.

Foreign markets were important for every automaker, but Willys was especially tied to overseas sales. *Fortune* magazine noted:

> For an independent, Willys-Overland is gunning for foreign business in a big way; indeed, with regard to export it is as daring and knowing as any of the Big Three. Even when its fortunes were at low ebb, Willys had a relatively high export quota—17 percent—and under its new program the allotment will be pushed to 25 percent, regardless of the range of local demand.

The station wagon underwent few significant changes during its long life, but improvements were incorporated along the way. The station wagon's horsepower problem was addressed in 1948 with the introduction of an optional six-cylinder engine. The flathead six displaced 148.5 ci and produced 72 horsepower and 117 foot-pounds of torque. A new, V-shaped face replaced the wagon's flat grille for 1950.

The station wagon's design was versatile enough for a Jeep pickup truck to spin off the platform in 1947 (see chapter 4). Brooks Stevens' melding of the Universal Jeep with other automotive forms probably reached its peak with the Jeepster Phaeton in 1948, a sort of car/Jeep hybrid that departed substantially from the pure utilitarian reputation of the Jeep (see chapter 4).

The 1953 CJ-3B had a curb weight of roughly 2,250 pounds, overall height of 67.75 inches, and overall length of 129.88 inches. The CJ-3B design has proved extremely durable. Besides being produced in the United States, the 3B has been built under license by Mitsubishi in Japan, Hotchkiss in France, and Mahindra in India.

Growing Up and Out

The Universal continued to evolve. The CJ-2A was produced into 1949, after which it gave way to the CJ-3A, which began trickling from factories in late 1948. The CJ-3A was not radically different from the 2A, but had a few distinguishing features. The CJ-3A utilized a one-piece windshield and was roughly 2 inches taller overall than the CJ-2A. The CJ-3A was strengthened by the employment of the Spicer 44 rear axle and revised front axle shaft.

As world events developed, a version of the CJ-3A would earn its own place in military history. At roughly the time CJ-3A production began running in earnest, the Korean War flared up, spurring production of a military version. Designated the M38,

this newest Jeep was built during 1950 and 1951. Willys-Overland produced 60,345 M38s during this time period.

The Korean War spawned the next generation of Jeep as well. Like the MB of World War II, the M38A1 made its debut as a military machine. As the M38's short life wound down, the M38A1 went into production in 1951. The M38A1, which would later be called the CJ-5 in civilian guise, addressed many of the original Jeep's shortcomings.

First, the A1 was much more comfortable than the Jeeps of the 1940s. It offered a better ride, thanks to 4-inch longer springs. It offered improved seating, since the M38A1's wider body gave soldiers more room than previous Jeeps. Its front fenders extended farther forward and were turned down at the leading edge, protecting soldiers from spray kicked up by the front tires. The M38A1 came with the new 72 horsepower F-head four-cylinder engine, boosting performance.

Variations of the M38A1 through the years included the M38A1C, which was essentially an M38A1 set up to carry a large, recoilless gun in its bed. The M38A1C's windshield had a large slot cut into it to allow the barrel of the gun to move up and down. The M170 (CJ-6 in civilian form) was used as a military ambulance. Between 1951 and 1963, 90,529 M38A1s were built.

Beating Plowshares into Toys

Many Jeeps were indeed put to work on farms, as officials in government and industry had predicted. But, increasingly, Jeep owners were purchasing Jeeps strictly for recreational purposes. With its four-wheel-drive capability and compact dimensions, the Jeep was perfect for scaling mountain passes or slogging through bottomlands on hunting trips, camping excursions, or a new type of activity, four-wheelin.'

In the late 1940s and early 1950s loose affiliations of Jeep enthusiasts began springing up around the country, especially in the western United States. Many of these affiliations formed clubs with regular off-roading events. The most famous and enduring of these Jeep events is the Jeepers Jamboree over the Rubicon Trail. Conceived in 1952, the Jeepers Jamboree takes participants over the Sierra Nevada Mountains across a rugged, boulder-strewn trail from Georgetown, California, to Rubicon Springs, near Lake Tahoe. With sections of the trail nicknamed the Big Sluice Box, Axle Rock, and The Cruncher, it is one of the toughest trails in the United States, and has developed an intensely loyal following.

Californians Mark Smith, Jim Sweeny, Jack Warner, Walt Drysdale, local Jeep dealer Ken Collins, Bill Hardie, Harold Krabbenhoft, and Gene Chappie dreamed up the Jamboree. These Jeep enthusiasts contrived the Jamboree as a way

Willys exited the U.S. passenger automobile market in 1955, making the CJ-5 the company's standard-bearer by default. Compared with the CJ-2A and CJ-3A, the CJ-5 was wider, had a larger windshield area, had 4-inch longer leaf springs for an easier ride, and softer seats. A hardtop was optional. The CJ-5 was built from 1955 until 1983. *Jeep photo*

Building an Aftermarket

From day one, the Jeep has been good to the automotive aftermarket industry. One of the first to capitalize on the Jeep's aftermarket potential was Warn Industries, maker of free-wheeling hubs, winches, and other off-road gear.

As owner of a Willys dealership in postwar Seattle, Arthur Warn had a close-up view of the Jeep from the beginning and knew the vehicle's strengths and weaknesses. One drawback was that the CJ-2A had no true two-wheel-drive setting. The transfer case could be disengaged, but the front axle was still locked, limiting fuel economy and drivability.

In 1947 Warn first developed small hubcaps that replaced the factory drive flanges. These hubcaps could be easily swapped on and off the front hubs in order to permit the CJ-2A to operate in two-wheel drive. Warn also offered a complete front axle conversion that replaced the front drive axle and transfer case, turning the Jeep into a true, full-time two-wheel-drive vehicle. In 1950 Warn developed his popular free-wheeling front hubs that easily switched from locked to unlocked with the simple locking ring.

Warn's endeavors later expanded to include a line of winches and other off-road hardware. But Warn Industries wasn't the only company to grow up with the Jeep. Regular off-roaders are familiar with enterprises such as the Ramsey Winch Company, Bestop, Dick Cepek Inc., and others largely through their efforts to improve those simple Jeep Universals.

to attract tourists to the Georgetown area, thus boosting the local economy. In 1952 these men, along with four others, piled into four Jeeps to scout out the proposed route.

The first Jamboree was held August 29 and 30, 1953. That year 55 vehicles and 155 people attended the two-day event, at $7.50 per person. The idea caught on quickly. For the second Jamboree 87 Jeeps carried 264 enthusiasts over the Rubicon. By the third year 130 Jeeps and 430 people made the trip. Growth was steady. By the 1980s and into the 1990s, the Rubicon Jeepers Jamboree routinely drew between 400

and 500 vehicles and 1,000 to 1,500 passengers.

Mark Smith, "Jeep Master" for that original excursion and for the following 39 years, remembers that the Jamboree attracted factory attention from the start. "In 1954 Willys came along; in fact a lot of their executives did," he said. At that time, the field was made up almost exclusively of CJ-2As.

"Ken Collins, who was a Jeep dealer in Placerville, he and I were friends," Smith said. "Ken, of course being a Jeep dealer, invited the people there from the factory." The Willys people all brought their own Jeeps, Smith said, and from there a long

relationship between the factory and the Rubicon Trail was established.

"When Kaiser acquired Jeep, Kaiser PR and many of the people from Kaiser, and, of course, their management, they came along too," Smith recalled. Cruse Moss, president of the automotive side of Kaiser-Frazer, even attended the Jamboree, Smith said. "In fact, Kaiser public relations—a fellow by the name of Alex Troffey—had *Life* magazine come along on the trip. *Life* covered it in 1957."

For factory representatives, the Rubicon wasn't just a joy ride. "I think actually we taught them what

Willys Motors released a number of bold ideas into the marketplace in an attempt to expand the Universal's appeal. The DJ-3A two-wheel drive chassis, introduced in 1956, was the basis for the Gala Surrey of 1959. Bedecked in two-tone pink paint, full-wheel hubcaps, striped seats, and striped top, the Gala Surrey was aimed at businesses that needed a specialized vehicle to ferry customers back and forth. The Surrey model returned in 1960 (shown) with expanded color choices. The replacement top on this Surrey lacks the pink stripes of the original, but is otherwise a fine example of the breed. *Photo courtesy Jim and Peg Marski Jeep collection*

the vehicles were capable of doing," Smith said. "The typical remark through the years has been 'If I hadn't seen the vehicle ahead of me [drive through] I would have turned around and gone back,' because they don't think it's possible. And of course one of the tricks there is driving without the clutch, and starting and stopping with the key only."

Eventually, the Rubicon Trail became, in its own way, a full-blown test track. "Actually, during the years, even when the CJ-7 came out, the introduction was done over the Rubicon Trail," Smith said. "And they would come out every year with something—running gear, just testing different suspension systems, things like that, through the years. That probably started around 1958, maybe 1960. And then as years went by it even increased more and more."

New Owners

If owner activity was taking off, so was corporate activity behind the scenes. During the 1950s many smaller, independent automakers either went under or merged with other small companies in an effort to stay afloat. Willys-Overland, never a giant to begin with, soon found itself in a David and Goliath position relative to the rest of the industry. After the initial sales boom from 1946 to 1948, Jeep sales dropped off in 1949 and 1950. This was partly because postwar demand for cars had largely been met, but also because the Korean War had dampened sales.

Although only semi-profitable in the early 1950s, the Jeep lineup of vehicles was still enticing—especially for automaker Kaiser-Frazer, which had been experiencing rough seas itself. In April 1953, during Willys-Overland's 50th anniversary year, Willys chairman Ward Canaday OK'd the sale of the company to Kaiser-Frazer Industries for $62 million. Kaiser became the first of many corporate owners to purchase the Jeep name. The Jeep side of the business was renamed Willys Motors.

That year saw new products as well. The newest Jeep was the CJ-3B, a clear offshoot of the Universal family, but with a distinctive difference. The CJ-3B featured a much taller hoodline to accommodate its more powerful 75- horsepower F-head four-cylinder engine.

The F-head stands in Jeep history looking both backward and forward. Whereas in the old flat-head arrangement both intake and exhaust valves were located in the engine block, in the F-head the

The Jeep utility wagon was a crucial part of Jeep's postwar strategy to diversify its product line while playing on the Universal's reputation. The wagon changed little over the years, from its 1946 introduction to its slow death in the mid-1960s. The 1962 model shown has the optional 226-ci L-head six-cylinder and optional front bumper rail and guards.

The station wagons maintained their simplicity through the years, but that was part of the appeal for many. Directional signals were optional.

intake valves were in the cylinder head, while the exhaust valves were still located in the block. The resulting taller cylinder head and split manifold arrangement made for a physically taller engine, necessitating a higher grille and hoodline. While functionally improved, the CJ-3B's body cast an odd shadow, with somewhat ungainly proportions. Strange looks or no, the CJ-3B was popular enough that it continued to be sold alongside other small Jeeps into the mid-1960s. The military version was designated the M606.

Hard on the CJ-3B's heels came the CJ-5, announced in October 1954 as a 1955 model. The CJ-5 retired the CJ-3A. The CJ-5 was the civilian version of the M38A1 introduced during the Korean War. Like its battlefield counterpart, the longer and wider CJ-5 offered more room and greater comfort than the CJ-2As and CJ-3As. The rear seat was wider

and the front seats were more comfortable. Styling diverged from the earlier look also, as the CJ-5 employed rounded fenders and a rounded hood.

Mechanically, the CJ-5 continued to use the F-head fourcylinder. The wheelbase was, at 81 inches, an inch longer than the CJ-2 and 3 series, with overall length increasing 6 inches and width 3 inches. The instrument cluster was redesigned and the glove compartment was available with a door. The CJ-5 had a fully boxed front cross-member for additional strength, and a larger windshield.

The new model expansion continued at a rapid clip under Kaiser. In 1956 a stretched wheelbase version of the CJ-5 was introduced, designated the CJ-6. The CJ-6's 101-inch wheelbase, 20 inches of extra sheet metal, and trucklike bed behind the front seats made it a lot more practical for industrial and commercial work. Compared to

The spare tire was carried in the cargo area of the wagon, eating into usable space. Although they were sold side-by-side for three years, the introduction of the 1963 Wagoneer killed sales of the utility wagon. The last year the utility wagon was the top of the Jeep line was 1962, when this example was built.

the CJ-5, the CJ-6 weighed roughly 150 pounds more, and cost $150 more. But the CJ-6 never quite caught on in the United States, and it rarely sold more than 2,500 copies a year while in production.

Also in 1956, a new two-wheel-drive Universal rolled out of Jeep factories, the DJ-3A Dispatcher. The DJ series retained the flat-fendered bodywork of the earlier CJ-3A (along with the older flathead four-cylinder engine) and was sold either open, with a unique canvas top, or with a hardtop. With its less complex drivetrain, the DJ-3A Jeeps cost nearly $400 less than a comparable CJ.

The Dispatcher Jeeps were targeted at a growing market, a market that had use for the Jeep's nimble size and open bodywork, but had no use for four-wheel-drive hardware. Specifically, the DJ was created with resorts, hotels, police departments, and later, the U.S. Postal Service in mind.

The DJ series was expanded in 1959 to include the Gala, which looked as if were designed to ferry fruity drinks back and forth between the hotel bar and beach. Along with a striped and fringed top, the Gala was sold in shocking colors, including a bright pink. From front-line military hero to cheery cabana boy, the Dispatcher Gala illustrated as well as anything the Jeep's postwar transformation. Almost no job was off-limits to the Jeep.

3

WORK DUTY: THE TRUCKS

It should be no surprise that a lineup of vehicles built around the rock-crawling, soldier-haulin' Jeep Universal would have room in its ranks for pickup trucks. To most people, Jeeps and pickups are merely different sides of the same coin. Both have difficult, dirty tasks to perform, but both are also used for recreation and good times. Both are ideal for transporting everything from wet dogs to deer carcasses. Both slug it out in the same corner of the marketplace.

Pickup trucks of one sort or another have carried the Jeep name since right after World War II. The first Jeep pickup was an offshoot of Brooks Stevens' station wagon design. Turning the station wagon into a pickup was a logical step, as the upright sheet metal and long wheelbase of the wagon were perfectly suited for a pickup. And since the two could share front sheet metal, it was an economical way to expand Willys-Overland's offerings. The Jeep pickup debuted as a 1947 model.

The Willys Jeep pickup was rated as either a 3/4-ton or 1-ton chassis. It was available as a pickup, or in chassis, chassis cab, and platform stake configurations. The 4x2 models used a solid front

In 1950, the Willys pickup truck received its first minor restyling, switching to a V-shaped grille with horizontal trim. Four-wheel-drive models like this one used a Spicer Model 18 transfer case, Spicer Model 25 full floating front axle, and Timken rear axle.

axle. With a 118-inch wheelbase the Jeep pickup was roughly the same size as most of its competitors. Its sharply folded sheet metal, however, set it apart from its more bulbous rivals, as did its Jeep Universal-inspired grille.

Initially the pickup was available only with the "Go-Devil" flathead four-cylinder engine, a distinct disadvantage considering most other trucks came standard with six-cylinder engines. Offsetting that was the fact the Jeep pickup was available, starting in July 1947, with factory four-wheel drive at a time when other truck makers relied on outside firms like Marmon-Herrington to offer four-wheel-drive conversions.

Competition for the Willys Jeep pickups came from Ford, Chevrolet, Dodge, GMC, Studebaker, and International Harvester. Generally, the Jeep pickup cost more than its competitors, but it was equipped with a rugged chassis

The pickup featured a simple, centrally mounted instrument cluster. The central location allowed Willys to easily construct either left-hand or right-hand drive models for export markets.

and drivetrain and was arguably better suited for hard work.

The Jeep also offered styling continuity, although whether that was a plus or a minus is open to debate. At a time when other pickup trucks seemingly changed sheet metal as frequently as a rattlesnake sheds its skin, the Jeep pickup retained most of its original styling well into the Mercury 7 age.

Yet internal changes were occasionally made. The 72-horsepower F-head four-cylinder replaced the 63-horse flathead midyear in 1950. In 1954, the year after Kaiser's purchase of Willys-Overland, the new owners made a well-received contribution in the form of a 226-ci L-head six. The 226, named the "Super Hurricane," produced 115 horsepower at 3,650 rpm, and 190 foot-pounds of torque at 1,800 rpm.

The first real styling change came in 1950. A V-shaped grille replaced the pickup's flat, Universal-type face. That grille was altered again for 1954, with three bright horizontal bars making the styling statement. A one-piece windshield replaced the old-fashioned split windshield in 1960. Two-tone paint combinations were a common method of keeping the pickup fresh through the years.

Late in the pickup's life, during the 1962 model year, Kaiser placed the overhead cam, 230-ci "Tornado" six-cylinder engine under truck hoods. Rated at 140 horsepower at 4,000 rpm, and 210 foot-pounds of torque at 1,750 rpm, the Tornado was a considerably more sophisticated engine than U.S. truck buyers were accustomed to seeing. Among other features, the six employed hemispheric combustion chambers and a chain-driven overhead cam- shaft. The OHC Tornado went on to power thousands of later Gladiator pickups and Wagoneers, but, unfortunately, the engine suffered from reliability problems and had a relatively short life.

The station wagon–based pickups had a long run, but after the Gladiator pickups were introduced for 1963 the original truck looked ancient by comparison. The two were sold together for a while, but the old stand-by was finally put to pasture in 1965.

Forward, March!

In 1957, the original pickup was joined by Jeep's most unusual truck ever—the Forward Control series. The Forward Control trucks were cab-over-engine designs. The high, forward-mounted cab provided good visibility for the driver when working in tight spaces, and a small turning radius. The configuration allowed for a relatively large

The Willys logo was featured prominently on the tailgate of early trucks. A Colorado fire department drafted the 1950 model shown, and equipped it with a fender-mounted siren and other relevant equipment.

truck bed on a short wheelbase. Jeep also touted the FC's low 27-inch bed height. Blessed with Jeep's four-wheel-drive hardware, the FC trucks were unique in the marketplace.

As Jeep showroom literature described it, " 'Up-front' visibility is a must for safe highway travel. Forward Control design lets you see the road six feet from the FC-170's front bumper. . . . Turn radius of 21 ft., 10 in. means easier all-around handling."

The Forward Control series initially was available in two models, the FC-150 and FC-170. The

short-wheelbase FC-150 (81-inch) was introduced first, in November 1956. The 104-inch wheelbase FC-170 version followed in the spring of 1957. Chassis and cab bodies were available from the start.

Besides overall length, there were significant differences between the two. The FC-150 came with the 134-ci, 72-horsepower F-head four-cylinder underhood; the Super Hurricane 226-ci, 105-horsepower straight six powered the FC-170. While a three-speed manual transmission was standard in both, a four-speed manual transmission was

ALL TRUCK...ALL OVER

2 WHEEL DRIVE "Jeep" Trucks set new marks for low-cost operation and maintenance. 4700-5300 lbs. gross vehicle weight. Functionally designed bodies in all popular styles.

When you see the new 2- and 4-wheel-drive "Jeep" Trucks at Willys-Overland dealers, you will spot feature after feature that make them great farm vehicles—a roomy cab with extra large windshield and windows . . . wide, full-opening hood for easier servicing . . . sturdy doors . . . fenders designed to

avoid damage and give access to wheels. With their rugged frames and the world-famous "Jeep" Engine, "Jeep" Trucks will give you years of service with low operating and maintenance expense. They are *all truck, all over*—engineered to serve you better and to **CUT YOUR HAULING COSTS.**

4 WHEEL DRIVE "Jeep" Trucks for the tough hauling jobs—off the road, through deep mud, up steep grades, over icy roads. 5300 lbs. gross vehicle weight. Power-take-off optional.

'Jeep' Trucks
CUT HAULING COSTS

WILLYS-OVERLAND MOTORS, TOLEDO   MAKERS OF AMERICA'S MOST USEFUL VEHICLES

The Willys Jeep pickup trucks shared most of their sheet metal with the station wagon. The flat grille was only seen on pickups for three years, 1947-1949. Although marketed as a Jeep truck, early examples, from the time when ownership of the "Jeep" name was still in dispute, carry only Willys markings.

optional on the FC-170. The FC-150 was rated at a Gross Vehicle Weight (GVW) of 5,000 pounds, while the FC-170's GVW was listed at 7,000 pounds.

The FC-170 was beefed up in 1959 with the addition of an optional heavy-duty rear end for the platform stake truck, which included "tougher full floating rear axle, heavy duty springs and shock absorbers, increased brake capacity and dual rear wheels," as Jeep literature described it. The heavy-duty setup raised GVW to 8,000 pounds, and up to 9,000 pounds on stake models with dual rear wheels and the four-speed transmission.

That year the FC-150 improved as well, with an increase in the width of the track, which resulted in more stable handling.

A three-cylinder Cerlist diesel–powered military version of the FC was built in the early 1960s. These vehicles were used primarily as ambulances and cargo trucks, and were delivered to the military in body styles that were never offered to the public.

The FC truck very nearly spun off a whole series of related vehicles. Designer Brooks Stevens whipped together several proposals for FC-based vans and other people movers that defied traditional categorization. But ultimately such plans were dismissed due to the FC's poor sales. The most popular year for the Forward Control trucks was the first, when 9,738 were produced. Most years annual production was about half that. The FC trucks were built until 1965, and quietly put to sleep. By then Jeep had figured out what General Motors, Ford, and Chrysler had discovered when they jumped into the market with their own forward control trucks in the early 1960s—when it comes to pickup trucks, Americans like them with a conventional layout: big hood, big fenders, big cab and big engine.

A Gladiator in the Arena

As long as the original Willys Jeep pickup lasted in the marketplace, the basic Gladiator/J-Series pickup managed to surpass even its longevity. Kaiser Jeep introduced the J-series Gladiator pickup for the 1963 model year, and it was produced, with running changes but in recognizable form, until the Chrysler purchase of AMC in 1987.

The Gladiator was an acknowledgment that the American truck market was moving away from its strictly agrarian roots. The newest trucks from Ford, Chevrolet, Dodge, and especially GMC featured sleek, slab-sided beds, ever-larger engines, and a lot more chrome trim than Grandpa was accustomed to seeing down on the farm. Vehicles like the Ford Ranchero and Chevy El Camino had helped further blur the line between car and truck. The Gladiator, with its sleeker lines, "Townside" step sided bed, more comfortable cab, and almost formal grille, represented one giant leap from the 1940s to the 1960s. In introductory advertisements, Jeep assured buyers "On the highway, it rides as smoothly as a passenger car."

Besides meeting the competition head-on, the Gladiator pickup's introduction also coincided with big changes at Jeep. In 1963 the company's name changed from Willys Motors to Kaiser-Jeep Corporation, to better reflect Kaiser's ownership. And the Gladiator pickup shared parts and sheet metal with the new Wagoneer introduced that year, a vehicle that was light years ahead of the older station wagon (see chapter six).

Like any American pickup worthy of the name, the Gladiator could be ordered in countless configurations. The J-200 and J-300 models were rated at 1/2-ton, 3/4-ton, or 1-ton, depending on how they were ordered. The J-200 rode on a 120-inch wheelbase and had a 7-foot bed, while the J-300's wheelbase measured 126 inches, and the bed 8 feet. Body choices included a traditional stepside, the "Thriftside," the slab-sided "Townside," a chassis and cab, or platform stake.

But the Gladiator didn't just mimic other pickups. It was quite technically innovative, as trucks go. It was certainly the only American truck with an overhead cam engine, the 230-ci Tornado six. And, at least at introduction, it was the only four-wheel-drive American pickup available with an automatic transmission and independent front suspension.

The Gladiator sold extremely well that first year, better than many people expected. It might have sold in even higher numbers initially had Kaiser offered an optional V-8. Engine choices did

The Forward Control Jeep trucks were available as either the short-wheelbase FC-150, or the long-wheelbase FC-170 (shown). The cab over engine design offered a great view immediately in front of the truck, but the prize was "unique" handling qualities. FC-170 models came standard with the six-cylinder "Super Hurricane" engine. FC-150s made do with a four-cylinder.

expand, starting with a lower-compression "economy" Tornado six in 1964, which produced 133 horsepower. The missing V-8 finally arrived for the 1965 model year.

Jeep's V-8 choice was a 327-ci engine rated at 250 horsepower. The V-8 came from an outside source, American Motors Corporation. The merging of Nash-Kelvinator and Hudson Motor Car Company in 1954 formed AMC. Like Willys-Overland and Kaiser, it had hoped to find new strength

Specifications, FC-170 (Forward Control)

wheelbase	103.5 in.
overall width	74 .5 in.
overall height	79.5 in.
overall length	181.5 in.
GVW	7,000 lbs. (8,000 lbs. and 9,000 lbs.) GVW optional)
tread	63.5 in.
curb weight	3,490 lbs.
transfer case	2-speed, ratio 1.00:1, 2.46:1
tires	7.00x16, 6-ply
pickup box	110 in. x 48.5 x 15.75
engine	226-ci L-head six-cylinder
horsepower	105 @ 3,600 rpm

meet the beautiful brute...

'JEEP' GLADIATOR

The Gladiator is the newest of the versatile, powerful, virtually indestructible 'Jeep' vehicles. On the highway, it rides as smoothly as a passenger car. Off the road, it's as sure-footed as only a 'Jeep' vehicle can be.

The Gladiator has the remarkable, new 140-horsepower Tornado-OHC engine. It's the *only* overhead camshaft engine in any American truck. Its higher torque at lower engine speeds makes light work of heavy loads. And it needs less maintenance, uses less fuel and will last longer than any comparable conventional engine.

It's easy to shift the Gladiator into 4-wheel drive. Just one knob does the job. Push it forward when you need extra traction, pull it back when you don't. Unique signal lights on the dashboard tell you when you're in 2- or 4-wheel drive.

You can have your Gladiator equipped with automatic transmission and independent front suspension. Don't waste time looking for other 4-WD trucks with these features. There aren't any.

It's the only 4-WD truck that can seat three comfortably. And in both step-in height and load height it's comparable to any truck. It's easy to step into, easy to load, yet it has traditional 'Jeep' ground clearance.

Choose the 'Jeep' Gladiator that suits you best...J-200 with 120-inch wheel base and 7-foot box, J-300 with 126-inch wheel base and 8-foot box. Choice of body styles with GVW's from 4000 to 8600 pounds. Step in. Size it up. Try it out at your 'Jeep' Dealer's.

all new all 'Jeep'

KAISER WILLYS MOTORS Willys Motors, world's largest manufacturer of 4-wheel drive vehicles, one of the growing Kaiser Industries.

The Gladiator pickup was new for 1963, available as a 1/2-ton, 3/4-ton, and 1-ton. GVW ratings ran from 4,000 to 8,600 pounds. The J-100 series and J-200 series rode on a 120-inch wheelbase and had a 7-foot bed; the J-300 series' wheelbase measured 126 inches and was teamed with an 8-foot bed. *Detroit Public Library, National Automotive History Collection*

Opposite: An ad from late 1962 pitched the new Gladiator as the "Beautiful Brute." This offering still shows Willys Motors as the company name. Shortly after the Gladiator's introduction, the company was renamed Kaiser Jeep.

Specifications, 1963 Gladiator J-200 Townside 4x4 pickup

wheelbase	120 in. (J-300, 126 in.)
curb weight	3,306 lbs.
tires	6.70x15 in.
engine	230-ci OHC six-cylinder
compression ratio	8.5:1
horsepower	140 @ 4,000 rpm
torque	210 foot-pounds @ 1,750 rpm

Get twice the "grip" of ordinary pick-ups with a 'Jeep' Gladiator.

Just flip one simple lever into 'Jeep' 4-wheel drive.

On the way to the building site, a 'Jeep' Gladiator handles like a passenger car. But once you're there, a simple shift puts you from 2-wheel to 4-wheel drive to take you right to the door—even before the driveway is in. Mud, snow, sand, even slippery streets—duck soup for this extra traction. Just shift into 'Jeep' 4-wheel drive at any speed, and you'll make calls, handle jobs you couldn't touch with an ordinary pick-up. All the usual options you'd expect. And you've

made a real investment, because Jeep' vehicles are backed by years of 4-wheel drive experience and know-how.

Equip your Gladiator to fit your needs: 250 hp V-8 engine or Hi-Torque 6; choice of colors; standard or custom cab and trim; full width or bucket seats; 3 power take-off points; 7 or 8-foot box; flat bed or stake with dual rear wheels; 3 or 4-speed transmission with standard shift, or Turbo Hydra-Matic* (it's the only pick-up offering automatic transmission with 4-wheel drive); power steering and power brakes available; GVW's 5000 to 8600 lbs. **KAISER Jeep CORPORATION** TOLEDO 1, OHIO

*TRADEMARK GENERAL MOTORS CORPORATION

You've got to drive it to believe it. See your 'Jeep' dealer. Check the Yellow Pages.

Kaiser Jeep pushed the Gladiator's four-wheel-drive capabilities in its advertising, as this piece from 1966 demonstrates. In 1966, the Gladiator was still the only pickup offering four-wheel drive and an automatic transmission.

in numbers, and the economical Rambler model did just that, carrying the company to prosperity in the late 1950s and early 1960s.

Breathing through a two-barrel Carter carburetor, the 327 was a fairly conventional overhead valve V-8 engine. It was used in the early and mid-1960s to power AMC's largest car, the Ambassador. This tie to AMC was expanded in 1967, when the innovative, but trouble-prone overhead cam, 230-ci six-cylinder was replaced with AMC's more traditional 232-ci overhead valve straight six. The 232 produced 145 horsepower.

Kaiser expanded its list of engine suppliers beyond AMC in the late 1960s to include Buick. First to appear was the "Dauntless" V-6 in CJs and Jeepster Commandos. The large Wagoneers and J-series trucks got the Buick 350-ci V-8 in 1969. Like the 327, a two-barrel carburetor topped it. The 350 was rated at 230 horsepower at 4,400 rpm, and 350 foot-pounds of torque at 2,400 rpm.

In 1970, Kaiser passed the keys of Jeep ownership to American Motors (outlined in greater detail in chapter 6). After AMC acquired Jeep it naturally began sliding its own engines underhood, further changing the personality of Jeep trucks. AMC's larger 258-ci six was made the standard engine for 1971. That same year the 360-ci V-8, rated at 175 net horsepower, replaced the Buick 350 as an option. The 304-ci V-8 became an option for 1972, tuned to 150 net horsepower. The largest AMC engine, the 401-ci V-8, arrived for 1974. Rated at 235 net horsepower, it remained an option until 1978.

The Gladiator's appearance changed as well, although not much. AMC gave the pickup a full-length grille for 1971, as had been done earlier with the Wagoneer. AMC dropped the Gladiator name in 1972. In 1973 the J-series pickup was given a long-overdue, double-wall bed, something most competitors had offered for years. The 1973 models also received a new dash and a Pioneer package with woodgrain trim, plush carpet, lots of chrome, and other luxuries. The Quadra-Trac full-time 4WD option came on line. Disc brakes were made available in 1974.

As the aging J-series pickup rolled through the 1970s, AMC tried its best to keep it relevant. One of the automotive fads to catch fire in the 1970s, as the last of the Detroit musclecars smoked their tires into the sunset, was the sport truck phenomenon. Jeep was one of the early arrivals in this arena. The prototypical sport truck was usually a step-side or short-bed model dolled up with mag wheels and garish graphics announcing the truck's sporting intentions. Aftermarket suppliers of such items as custom wheels, CB radios, driving lights, stripe kits, and the like sent a generation of kids to college off the proceeds, and the factories wanted in on the action.

Jeep's entry was labeled the Honcho, and it was labeling that was hard to miss. The Honcho arrived

When the Jeepster Commando series was introduced in late 1966, it was available as a convertible, station wagon, roadster, or half-cab pickup. Like the Jeep Universal, the Commando pickup was rated as a 1/4-ton chassis, with a GVW of 3,550 pounds. Setting the Commando pickup apart from its competitors (with the exception of the International Scout utility pickup) was its standard four-cylinder engine. The new Dauntless V-6 was optional, as was a Turbo-Hydramatic automatic transmission. *Detroit Public Library, National Automotive History Collection*

in 1976 on the J-10. Equipment included fender flares, large tires and wheels, "Honcho" billboard graphics, and a sport steering wheel. A Laredo package joined it on the option list. A roll bar later became a standard part of the Honcho package.

AMC tried to work a little fuel economy magic on the J-series trucks in the early 1980s, an optimistic endeavor at best. In 1980 the engineers went through the Jeep drivetrain components, slashing weight where practical. AMC fit the J-trucks with a standard air dam in 1981 to clean up the airflow underneath the pickup. The sunshade lip over the windshield was retired that year as well.

A new part-time Selec-Trac four-wheel- drive system replaced the Quadra-Trac full-time four-wheel-drive system for 1983. The Selec-Trac system was optional on J-10s with automatic transmissions. The Selec-Trac used a "viscous drive controlled slip differential for smooth quiet operation," as company literature described it. The system offered a simple dash switch for changing from two-wheel drive to four-wheel drive, with a transfer case lever on the floor for shifting between 4WD high and 4WD low.

Near the end of the J-Series pickup's long life, it settled into a niche. Its unique sheet metal and rugged four-wheel drive persona set it apart from most other pickups. *Car and Driver* magazine summed it up in the 1982 Buyers Guide:

> *Heavy Duty!* We have here your basic kick-ass, bun-busting, big-time pickup trucks. There is no question of intent or malice aforethought. These devices are intended to haul the mail through hell or high water. It's their bound'n duty.

That niche had begun to shrivel as the 1980s progressed, though, thanks to high gas prices. Japanese automakers Toyota and Datsun made huge inroads into the American market with fuel efficient, compact pickups, dragging the truck market in that direction. The heavyweight J-series truck coexisted with its compact replacement, the Comanche, for a brief period, but was retired thereafter. Production of the J-trucks ended September 30, 1987. The smaller, quicker lightweights were knocking the big guys around in the sales ring.

A Traditional Approach

Before killing the J-series pickup and giving birth to the Comanche, Jeep tried to bridge the gap between big and small using the reliable CJ series as a base. Debuting for the 1981 model year, the CJ-8, or Jeep Scrambler, was reminiscent of the CJ-6 but was clearly intended to be used as a pickup truck rather than just a stretched Jeep Universal.

AMC sought to position the Scrambler as an American alternative to compact Japanese 4x4 pickups. "Jeep Scrambler . . . America's first small 4x4 pickup," the showroom brochure read. "Once you drive Jeep Scrambler you may never go back to an ordinary small truck again. Nothing else looks like . . . nothing else performs like Scrambler. It's a go-almost-anywhere-under-the-sun fun or work machine." Ultimately, however, with its rough-and-tumble personality, stark interior, and four-wheel-drive running gear, the Scrambler proved more attractive to traditional Jeep owners than to import pickup buyers.

The Scrambler rode on a wheelbase that was 10 inches longer than that of the CJ-7 and it was 2 feet longer overall. Like the CJ-7, the Scrambler featured a prominent roll bar, which was mounted in its 5-foot bed. Payload was rated at 1,400 pounds. The 82-horsepower 2.5-liter (151-ci) four-cylinder was the standard engine, with the 4.2-liter six optional. The Scrambler was available with a soft-top or hardtop, making it America's only convertible truck.

Car and Driver magazine zeroed in on the Scrambler's strengths in its July 1981 issue. "The most important benefits of this long-wheelbase chassis are felt on the highway, where the Scrambler brings a long-awaited dose of refinement to pavement Jeeping," the article noted. "Unlike the CJ-5 and CJ-7, the Scrambler doesn't pitch back and forth like a yearling saddle bronc over Interstate expansion strips."

The Scrambler could be configured three ways: the base model (open body), the SR Sport, or the SL Sport. The SR Sport package included denim vinyl high-back bucket seats; bold graphics along the rockers and front fenders; a Scrambler hood decal; the "soft feel" three-spoke steering wheel; a day/night mirror; L78x15 outlined white letter tires; and an underhood light, as well as a few other dress-up items. The SL Sport was the top of the line, offering buyers a leather-wrapped steering wheel, chrome bumpers and grille, P235/75R15 Wrangler tires, its own distinct striping, a tachometer and clock, a console, carpeting, and other niceties. These trim levels were replaced by the Renegade and Laredo packages in 1985.

The Scrambler was produced through 1985. Although held in high regard by collectors today, less than 28,000 were ever built. Its best year was its first, 1981. Although a unique solution to the mini-truck problem, the Scrambler faced tough competition from the new Chevrolet S-10 and Ford Ranger compact pickups, plus very good offerings from Toyota, Datsun, and Mazda.

The Last Truck

Jeep's entry into the compact truck market arrived in the fall of 1985 as a 1986 model. The new truck was named Comanche, and compared to other small pickups, it was quite unique. The Comanche shared not only the Cherokee's front sheet metal, but also its unibody construction—an unusual trait, as most pickups utilized body-on-frame construction. The Comanche had a solid front axle with coil springs, instead of the more common independent front suspension. And for a compact the Comanche was a bit on the chunky side, being slightly longer than its Ford Ranger

The Honcho J-series pickup represented AMC's attempt to break into the sport truck market. The 1977 Honcho package, as shown, was available on the J-10. It included colorful Honcho graphics, large Goodyear Tracker tires, 10 x 15 white spoke wheels, and a sport steering wheel. It was a $749 option that year. Honcho stripe treatment varied from year to year. *Detroit Public Library, National Automotive History Collection*

and Chevrolet S-10 competition. Initially the Comanche was sold only on a 119-inch wheelbase as a long-bed model.

The base engine was the 2.5-liter four-cylinder with throttle-body fuel injection. Optional was a 2.8-liter V-6, supplied to AMC from General Motors. AMC also offered an optional 2.1-liter intercooled turbo diesel four-cylinder. The Comanche could be ordered with either Command-Trac or Selec-Trac four-wheel-drive systems.

The Comanche was sold in a Base model, an X model, and the XLS, although option packages shifted frequently during the Comanche's life. Pioneer, Comanche Chief, and Laredo packages soon supplanted the X-models. The Eliminator was introduced as the sport truck model for 1988, available on two-wheel- drive shortbeds.

Most reviews of the new Comanche were favorable. "The Comanche has a solid, refined feel," noted

Pete Lyons in *Car and Driver's* October 1985 issue:

Ride, handling, and stability are all good both on-road and off (which is quite a trick), and the front suspension's non-independence is undetectable. Some drivers may find the bucket seat design a little cramped and the steering wheel a little too close, but otherwise the cabin environment is very acceptable.

Underhood help arrived in 1987, when a much-improved fuel-injected, 4.0-liter inline six replaced the underachieving 2.8-liter V-6. With 177 horsepower, the Comanche was the most powerful compact truck available in America. A shortbed version on a 113-inch wheelbase further fleshed out the lineup in 1987.

While many a past Jeep had earned racing glory crashing through the desert at the Baja 1000, the Comanche carved out an unusual racing history for itself. The Sports Car Club of America (SCCA) created the Racetruck Challenge shortly

The CJ-8, also known as the Scrambler, arrived for 1981 and was sold until 1985. The CJ-8 was a useful all-around vehicle, offering the CJ's off-road capability along with a modest pickup bed and the smoother ride that a longer wheelbase provided. But as a pickup, the Scrambler was on the small side. Its cargo box measured 61.5 inches long and 55.8 inches wide, compared to 83.6 inches long and 68 inches wide for the short-wheelbase J-10. The 1983 Scrambler, as shown, was available as an open body base model, as an SR Sport, or as an SL Sport.

after the Comanche's birth. This road racing series pitted compact pickups against one another from 1987 to 1991. Compact trucks were at the peak of their late twentieth century popularity, and a racing series to showcase the vehicles seemed timely. The Comanche raced against the Ford Ranger, Chevy S-10 GMC S-15, Dodge D50, and pickups from Toyota, Nissan, and Mitsubishi. To keep costs low, four-cylinder versions of the trucks were approved by the rules for competition.

The Archer brothers, Tommy and Bobby, were the main Jeep hotshoes. They led Jeep to the Racetruck manufacturers' championships in 1987 and 1988. Tommy Archer captured the driver's championship in 1988. During the series' five-season run, the Jeep Comanche finished at a tie for second with the Ford Ranger for most victories by make (14). Nissan trucks scored the most wins (16).

The Comanche's final year was 1992. By then the Power Tech 4.0-liter six's output had swollen to 190 horsepower. And the option list allowed buyers to pack the Comanche with as many luxuries as more expensive trucks offered, but sales had nonetheless been in steady decline. The decision to end the Comanche's life came from a combination of two factors—low sales and Chrysler's attempts to make the Jeep brand fit into the Chrysler hierarchy of Plymouth, Dodge, and Chrysler. The ideal solution, in the eyes of many at Chrysler, was to make the Jeep the sport utility division, while all trucks were to be sold under the Dodge umbrella. Dodge already had the full-size Ram, the mid-size Dakota, and the compact Mitsubishi-built Ram 50. Why sell another rival from within the corporation?

Many Jeep dealers, particularly those in truck-crazy states such as Texas and California, were at a loss without a pickup to sell. To them, corporate strategies were fine and all, but the end result was that they had no pickup to sell at a time when trucks were attracting record numbers of customers. It's only speculation, but had Chrysler offered an extended cab Comanche, or shifted the Comanche name to a Grand Cherokee–based pickup, we might still be able to purchase a Jeep pickup today.

4

TWO GENERATIONS: THE JEEPSTERS

On the surface (and according to collectors of the two), the two generations of vehicles to share the Jeepster name do not have much in common. The first Jeepsters, built in the late 1940s and early 1950s, are as distinct from the 1960s-era Jeepsters as a Shelby Mustang is from a Shelby Charger. And yet both attempt to attack the same problem from a similar angle. Both attempt to somehow fuse traditional Jeep characteristics of ruggedness and simplicity with the smooth ride, comfort, and convenience of an automobile. That and a nameplate comprise the tenuous thread that binds the two together.

The early Jeepsters, like the station wagon and first Willys Jeep trucks, sprang from the fertile pen of designer Brooks Stevens. The task was to create a more car-like vehicle that played on the Jeep name, without breaking the corporate bank in the process. The Jeepster shared a face reminiscent of the Jeep Universal's, and was powered by the standard Jeep engine. Beyond that, it did not have much in common with its war-bred relative.

To cut costs, the Jeepster shared much with the Willys station wagon and pickup. The grille, hood, and front fenders came from the wagon and pickup parts bin, although Willys dressed it up with the waterfall trim on the grille. The four-cylinder 1949 Jeepster, as shown, had not greatly changed from the 1948 models. One improvement for 1949, though, was the availability of a six-cylinder engine.

The stylized Willys "W" was prominently featured on the Jeepster hood. There was more room for such small extras in the market the Jeepster was trying to reach, which was not the case with the Jeep Universal.

The stylistic Willys "W" carried over into the interior of the Jeepster. Gauges and the steering wheel were also shared with the station wagon. The Jeepster interior featured a fold-and-tumble passenger seat.

Instead, the Jeepster was an offshoot of the station wagon and pickup lineage. Introduced on April 3, 1948, the Jeepster shared its suspension and a lot of its sheet metal with the wagon. The grille, hood, and front fenders were standard-issue station wagon pieces. The Jeepster was built on the station wagon and pickup chassis, although an X-brace stiffened the frame to keep the open phaeton body style from twisting excessively.

The "Go-Devil" flathead four-cylinder engine was the only powerplant available initially, although an overdrive transmission helped it along. All Jeepsters utilized a black or gray top with a tan underside, and side curtains instead of roll-up windows. As with the open Jeep Universal, carpeting would have been silly, so Jeepsters were sold with

rubber floor mats. The front passenger seat could be folded completely forward to allow access to the rear seat.

The major divergence the Jeepster took from other Jeeps was its availability in two-wheel- drive form only. This was in keeping with Willys-Overland's attempts to create a new kind of vehicle, one that traded on the Jeep name without being pigeon-holed into a particular category. As print advertisements attempted to explain it:

There's a singing joyful way about this car. There's also a lack of dead weight . . . an absence of stale ideas in automotive design. The Jeepster is refreshing and new and *fun*. The only thing like it is another Jeepster. And this year, many people like you are going to make that happy discovery.

Fun may have been the Jeepster's reason for existence, but with only a flathead four-cylinder under the hood, it was a pale sort of fun. This was remedied in July 1949, when Willys-Overland's flathead 148-ci "Lightning" six-cylinder was added to the option list. Rated at 72 horsepower and 117 foot-pounds of torque at 1,600 rpm, it slightly bettered the L-head four's 63 horsepower and 105 foot-pounds of torque at 2,000 rpm.

The carpet was yanked from under the flathead four-cylinder for 1950, when the 72-horsepower F-head four-cylinder was added to the lineup. The F-head made its extra power through better breathing. Whereas the flathead arrangement placed both intake and exhaust valves in the block, the F-head design moved the intake valves into the cylinder head. The F-head also boasted a slightly higher compression ratio.

The six-cylinder's displacement was punched out to 161 ci in 1950, although horsepower was up only marginally, to 75. But the sixes were a rarity under Jeepster hoods. In two years of production only 2,433 Jeepsters were built with the engine. Despite the attempted power fixes, the Jeepster's performance was still on the sluggish side.

The Jeepster came with rear fender steps to help along back-seat passengers, although those steps were no small reach. A rear bumper-mounted spare was standard equipment.

Fun was the catchword for the new Jeepster. Willys was still feeling its way forward when it came to marketing the postwar Jeep products. This ad is somewhat of a departure, in that it does not try to link the Jeepster to the Willys' military contributions.

In ads and press photos, Willys-Overland didn't hesitate to position the 1948 Jeepster in high-class settings. Willys tried to convince buyers the Jeepster was suitable for fun, informal activities, but also for times when a fur coat was the apparel of choice. *Jeep photo*

For 1950 the Jeepster was given a V-shaped grille with horizontal trim. The interior was revised that year as well, with a new instrument panel. The 1950 models were the final Jeepsters in the original series; 1951 models were leftover 1950s.

The Jeepster received its first styling revisions in 1950. The 1950 model details included a new V-shaped grille with horizontal crossbars and a new instrument panel. The earlier cars' rectangular panel with square speedometer and surrounding instruments was replaced by a panel featuring a large, round, centrally located speedometer, with the fuel, oil, amp, and coolant temperature gauges in a line below it. One interesting idea never put into production was that of a more car-like Jeepster hardtop. Alcoa, purveyors of all things aluminum, developed a prototype Jeepster-based car, but it was never put into production.

With World War II receding a safe distance in the rearview mirror and Americans eager to replace their aging prewar cars, Willys hoped there would be room in the marketplace for unusual vehicles like the Jeepster—especially vehicles that could be manufactured on the cheap. Many in the U.S. auto industry noticed that sports car sales were growing

steadily in the United States (an acknowledgment that later led to the Chevrolet Corvette and Ford Thunderbird). Makes such as MG and Triumph had captured the interest of American GIs stationed in Europe during the war. As a result, many brought such cars home from Europe or were buying freshly imported examples. Perhaps the Jeepster would appeal to some of them was the thinking.

But the Jeepster was not a true sports car, lacking both a sufficiently sporty suspension and powerful engine. What's more, it was not quite a true Jeep either, lacking off-road capabilities. It was a fun, open car, but that was not particularly unique. Virtually every manufacturer at the time offered convertibles. As a vehicle, the Jeepster didn't fit into any easily recognized, comfy category.

Its relatively high price also hurt the Jeepster. Other new postwar cars started arriving in showrooms in 1948, and most of them offered convertible tops with roll-up windows, more trunk space,

The Commando station wagon model came with a full top, and was priced at $2,749 in 1967. Although the front sheet metal was similar in appearance to that of the CJ-5, the Jeepster Commando had its own distinct hood and grille. The wider hood nearly swallowed the fenders, while the wider grille allowed placing the parking lamps outboard of the headlamps.

The top-of-the-line Jeepster in 1967 was the convertible (shown), with prices starting at $3,186. The Jeepster offered more luxuries than the Universal, including an optional power top. A stripped-down model sold without a top was marketed as the Roadster.

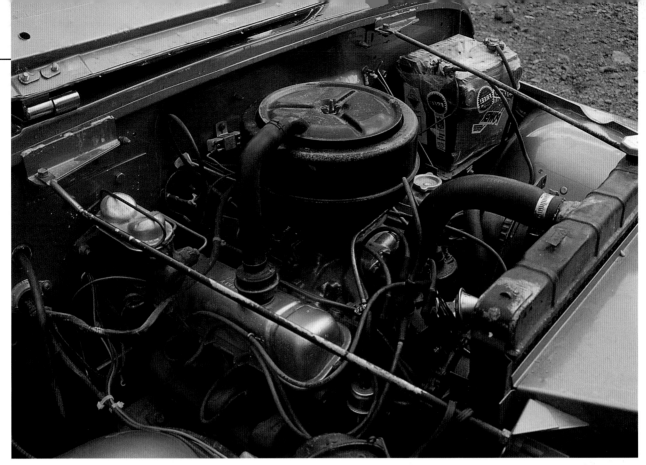

The F-head four-cylinder was the base engine in the Jeepster, but the Dauntless V-6 was a popular option. Supplied by Buick, the 225-ci Dauntless was available in Jeeps from 1966 to 1971.

and more power. The Jeepster, meanwhile, offered no price advantage compared to traditional Ford or Chevy convertibles.

Production of the original Jeepster ended after 1950. A few 1951 models were registered, but these were merely leftover 1950 models. Although unique in its time, and beloved today by organizations such as the Willys-Overland Jeepster Club, the Jeepster was Willys' first postwar failure. But the name and the concept would live to try another day.

A Sixties Commando

When the Jeepster name was revived in the late 1960s, the vehicle to which it was attached shared much more in common with the Jeep Universal than the earlier Jeepster. Even though it was somewhat compromised compared to the CJ-5, the Jeepster Commando was more a true "Jeep." It came equipped with four-wheel drive and much of the heavy-duty hardware available on the tough Universals.

There was also greater variety of body styles. The Jeepster Commando was sold as an open roadster, a

station wagon, a convertible, and a half-cab pickup. Although the Commando represented no revolutionary breakthrough, it was the first compact four-wheel drive utility vehicle available with an automatic transmission. Its power top was unique in its class.

Its optional V-6 engine was a departure from the traditional inline sixes. The 225-ci "Dauntless" six had been introduced in the 1966 Universals, and was an ideal engine for the Jeepster Commando. Rated at 160 horsepower, the V-6 offered good power in a compact package. Buick had originally developed the engine, and it was introduced in the company's 1962 Special line at 198 ci. In 1964 Buick increased the displacement to 225 ci. But the V-6 was abandoned by GM's upscale division, as the 1960s' march toward ever more powerful V-8 engines left it wheezing at the back of the pack. Kaiser purchased the tooling from Buick in the mid-1960s and gave the engine a solid home in the smaller Jeep products.

These unique features were important for the Jeepster Commando, as competition was much fiercer in the utility vehicle market of the 1960s than in previous decades. International Harvester's Scout, introduced in 1961, had quickly established a loyal following. Ford's Bronco was new for 1966, and benefited from the huge Ford dealer network. Both makes offered open cab, station wagon, and half-cab pickup models.

Kaiser gave the Jeepster Commando one other advantage over the original Jeepster—better promotion. Kaiser released 600 Jeepster Commandos in 1966 as promotional models to garner attention before the official January 1967 rollout. The first television ads for the Commando appeared on *Candid Camera* in early 1967, and many more followed. Print ads were much more plentiful than in the original Jeepster's day.

What potential buyers found when they wandered into Jeep showrooms was a new form of Jeep that sat on a 101-inch wheelbase, compared to the CJ-5's 81 inches. The front sheet metal looked like it came straight from the CJ-5, but the Commando had its own wider grille and hood. Sitting atop the Jeepster Commando's longer wheelbase was a longer body with more overhang. This offered the advantages of more cargo space, greater passenger comfort, and a smoother ride, but also handicapped the Commando off-road. The smaller wheelwells and lower-hanging sheet metal meant it was more difficult to fit the Commando with larger tires, and also that the vehicle was more likely to drag body panels against the usual boulders and logs found on rough trails. Additionally, the Commando was fitted from the factory with street tires and full-face hubcaps, whereas the CJ came with knobbier rubber.

The F-head 134-ci four-cylinder with a three-speed transmission was the standard powertrain, with the V-6 optional. Prices for the least-expensive Commando started at $2,466 for the Roadster. The convertible model was on the pricey side, starting at $3,186. CJ-5 prices started at $2,361.

Sales of the new Jeepster Commando were not record breaking, but were in keeping with other similar vehicles of the type. Most years, sales of the Commando, Bronco, and Scout settled into a clip of 10,000-15,000 units per year. The Commando helped Kaiser flesh out the Jeep line at a time when competition was growing fiercer.

For the first few years of production, changes to the Jeepster Commando were few. In 1968, alterations in trim and hubcaps marked the limit of changes to the Commando for that year. As per federal regulation, side marker lamps were included for 1969.

AMC's purchase of Jeep in 1970 signaled new directions ahead for the Commando, although not

Willys-Overland Jeepster Production	
1948	10,326
1949	2,961
1950	5,845*
Total	19,132

* 1951 models were leftover 1950 models, and are included in this total.

Kaiser/AMC Jeepster and Commando Production (calendar year)	
1966	2,345
1967	12,621
1968	13,924
1969	11,289
1970	9,268
1971	7,903
1972	10,685
1973	9,538
Total	77,573

George Hurst became a bit of a celebrity in automotive circles in the late 1960s, thanks to his shifters, wheels, and special edition cars. His best-known collaboration was with Oldsmobile. The Hurst/Olds 442 is remembered as one of the fastest muscle cars of its time. The Hurst Special Jeepster is lucky to be remembered at all.

Although slathered in musclecar styling cues, a humble V-6 powered the Hurst Special Jeepster. With approximately 100 examples built, the Hurst Special Jeepster is among the rarest Jeeps ever made.

immediately. Scarcely anyone saw one of the first changes brought to the Commando. In 1971, AMC OK'd a special edition Hurst Jeepster Commando. AMC had worked previously with Hurst, an aftermarket company best known for its high-performance shifters, wheels, and other musclecar-era paraphernalia. AMC had collaborated with Hurst on the 1969 SC/Rambler, the 1969 SS/AMX, and the 1970 Rebel Machine, and had garnered good notice in the press with these musclecar special editions.

But the Hurst Jeepster Special was a mixed bag. It contained many musclecar styling cues at a time when musclecars were starting on the path to extinction. And while the looks promised perfor-

mance, the Hurst Jeepster Special was still just a utilitarian Jeep under the skin. Hurst Jeepster equipment included the 225-ci V-6 with 2-barrel carb, rated at 160 horsepower; a fiberglass hood incorporating a large scoop with built-in tach; a Hurst three-speed manual T-shifter or Hurst dual-gate shifter if the optional automatic transmission was ordered; rally stripes; and Hurst identification.

Best estimates indicate that perhaps 100 were built, at most. Even if the Hurst Special didn't make a huge splash in the marketplace, it is at least significant as the last vehicle produced with Hurst/AMC collaboration. Its rarity has also made it one of the most collectible Jeeps.

larger, more comfortable utility vehicles that would be the theme for the 1970s.

Although they were quite different in size and price, *Motor Trend* compared the Blazer with the Bronco and the Jeepster in its June 1971 issue. "In our little contest the Blazer wins hands down with the Bronco a distant second," said Chuck Koch. "Although the name Jeep is synonymous with four-wheel drive, the Jeepster Commando was more of a combination street/dirt car, not really suited for really rough off-roading," the article noted. "Its suspension is too soft and ground clearance not sufficient to surmount large obstacles. On our trip, though, it did go where the Blazer and Bronco went but with more difficulty." With the smallest engine of the bunch the Jeepster recorded the best mileage (13.5 miles per gallon), and was judged second-most comfortable behind the Blazer, but clearly the large two-door utility vehicle had arrived and was making friends fast.

Not surprisingly, the Hurst Jeepster sported a Hurst Dual-Gate shifter between its bucket seats when optioned with the automatic transmission. The base transmission was a three-speed manual with Hurst T-handle shifter.

A more modest Jeepster Commando sport model accompanied the Hurst edition in 1971. The SC-1 option adorned the Commando with body-length SC-1 stripes and full wheel covers, plus other special trim.

At the time, though, the Hurst Jeepster and SC-1 were shooting at the wrong target. Musclecar influences were not as effective as they had been a few short years before, and the utility vehicle market was developing rapidly. The introduction of the Chevrolet Blazer exemplified the trend toward

Much like the musclecars it sought to emulate, the Hurst Jeepster sported a hood-mounted tachometer.

AMC's influence became a lot more obvious with the introduction of the 1972 Jeepster Commando. The revised front end was a clear departure from earlier Jeep designs, more reminiscent of Chevrolet's Blazer than the traditional Jeep Universal. Under the skin, AMC's straight six replaced the Dauntless V-6. This Commando has the optional 304-ci V-8.

Besides the new sheet metal, the 1972 Jeepster Commando rode on a longer wheelbase—104 inches, compared to the previous 101 inches.

AMC's Influence

As AMC worked to bring Jeep into the corporate fold, the Jeepster began showing more signs of the ownership switch. For 1972, the Commando (the Jeepster tag was dropped) was revamped, with what was perhaps the most uncharacteristic Jeep styling of any product to wear the badge in a decade. The new front-end sheet metal mimicked the look of Chevrolet's popular Blazer, discarding the traditional vertically slotted Universal face in favor of a stamped, egg crate–type grille. The 1972 models were longer, riding on a 104-inch wheelbase.

That year also saw the phasing in of AMC's engines. The four-cylinder and V-6 were dropped, with the 232-ci AMC inline six designated the standard engine. It produced 100 net horsepower at 3,600 rpm. One welcome addition was an optional 304-ci, two-barrel V-8, rated at 150 horsepower. With the extra power and weight added, AMC engineers gave the Jeepster larger brakes for 1972.

The SC option returned, this year updated to SC-2. An SC-2 equipped with the optional V-8 qualified as a sporty model in more than just name.

The final year for the second-generation Jeepster was 1973. It was given larger tires, but there were few other changes that year. Sales had gone soft, and it had become apparent that the market was moving in two directions. The trend was toward the larger, more luxurious utilities (Dodge introduced a full-size, two-door utility named the Ramcharger in 1974, and Ford up-sized the Bronco in 1978), and the nimble, small utilities like Jeep's own CJ. There was little middle ground.

The Jeepster name may yet live again. Chrysler proposed a possible third generation Jeepster in concept car form in 1998. This Jeepster was a technical showcase, and had a whiff of the modern-day musclecar about it, with a 4.7-liter, 32-valve V-8 engine, electronic four-wheel independent suspension, and aggressively styled body. In the truck-happy early twenty-first century, there seems to be plenty of room for middle ground.

A smoother ride and more legroom were selling points when the Commando was revamped for 1972, although reminders of Jeep's traditional toughness were never ignored. The Blazer-influenced grille of the long-wheelbase Commando only saw the light of day for two years, 1972 and 1973.

5

THE SPOTLIGHT SHINES BRIGHTER:
THE 1960S, 1970S, AND A TOUCH OF THE 1980S

The 1960s is a decade usually remembered for the social and cultural changes that occurred in America, but the period was a pretty rollicking good time for any manufacturer of trucks or utility vehicles. This less glamorous side of the business world grew with great abandon as automakers expanded choices and did a better job of making the vehicles more livable for daily use. In 1960 total U.S. truck and bus production stood at 1,202,011 vehicles. By 1969 that total had swollen to 1,981,519. By way of comparison, in 1950 truck and bus production was 1,377,261 units, higher even than in 1960.

Momentum behind these capable machines had been growing for some time. Other American automakers began crowding the traditional Jeep territory in the late 1950s. Chevrolet began offering factory four-wheel- drive pickups in 1957, and Ford followed suit in 1959.

The Renegade I made its first appearance in 1970. A limited edition model, the Renegade's visual impact was made with the eye-catching purple or green colors. The Renegade I came with simple 8-inch-wide wheels; the example shown has aftermarket mags.

With its short wheelbase and light weight, the CJ-5 was the perfect base for a sport Jeep model like the Renegade I.

Renegade models came with a roll bar long before it became standard throughout the CJ line. The Renegade was a sport model intended to remind the public of the racing Jeeps of Baja fame.

The Renegade was available with extra oil and amp gauges. The dash-mounted ID tag shows this limited edition Jeep was built in April 1970. CJ-5s were never sold with automatic transmissions.

If the Super Jeep looked like something Evel Knievel would drive on a date with Charlie's Angels while his Trans-Am was in the shop, it was only a sign of the times. The 1973 Super Jeep came with rubber lip extensions on the fenders, a roll bar, chrome front bumper, painted wheels, and those wild graphics. The six-cylinder engine was standard, the V-8 optional. Although advertisements usually depicted red, white, and blue Super Jeeps, the graphics were available in several color combinations.

and powerful for a six, the OHC Tornado soon proved itself less than rock-solid reliable. It was also more difficult to work on than more common overhead valve pushrod engines. And buyers of this class of vehicle usually liked a choice. A Wagoneer could be expected to climb mountain trails, tow boats, slog down snowy highways, and everything imaginable in between. Competitors like Chevrolet had an optional 283-ci V-8 available in the Suburban Carryall, and if Jeep executives expected to maintain momentum with the Wagoneer they would need to match that capability.

An attempt to expand the engine offering came in 1964, although this expansion was probably in

the wrong direction. Jeep added an "economy" 230 OHC six to the engine list. With a lower compression ratio, the engine produced 133 horsepower. True help didn't arrive until 1965, when a 327-ci V-8 was added to the option list. American Motors Corporation supplied the 327. AMC would, in due course, supply more than just an engine. Rated at 250 horsepower, a two-barrel carburetor fed the 327.

Development of the Wagoneer continued steadily. In December 1965 Jeep released the Super Wagoneer. In 1966 the four-door Wagoneer was given a new grille and a slotted face that ran from fender to fender, and incorporated the headlights

After years as a special limited edition, in 1974 the Renegade became a regular production model. AMC's 304-ci V-8 was part of the package, as was the roll bar, passenger grab handle, dual sun visors, oil and amp gauges, slotted mag wheels, heavy-duty cooling, special paint, and a rear-mounted spare tire. Jeep photo

Initially created in 1970 as a limited edition CJ-5, and later a regular production model, the Renegade name was also given to the CJ-7 series after the larger Universal's 1976 introduction. Shown is a 1977 CJ-7 Renegade. In the late 1970s AMC paid more attention to comfort and convenience, as items like air conditioning made the option list.

in a CJ-6. For most of the early years the Bronco was the Jeep's main competition, thanks to the efforts of Ford veteran Bill Stroppe.

More competition arrived in the 1960s from a new source—Toyota. The Japanese automaker began shipping its FJ-25 Land Cruiser utility vehicles to the United States in 1957. Perhaps more than any other, this lineup of vehicles followed the Jeep blueprint. The FJ-25 was a two-door, soft-top four-wheel-drive utility vehicle powered by a 3.8-liter gasoline six. It was sold in the United States until 1959, after which Toyota shipped in its replacement, the capable FJ-40. The two-door FJ-40 was exported from Japan to the United States from roughly 1960 until 1984, and in that time developed a loyal following of its own. Toyota's 55-series Land Cruiser station wagon arrived in the United States in the late 1960s, giving the Wagoneer an unwelcome competitor. The two-door FJ-series Land Cruiser disappeared in the United States long ago, but the larger Land Cruiser wagon remains a competitor of the Grand Cherokee to this day.

Chevrolet attacked from a different angle in 1969 with its two-door Blazer, a vehicle that most closely resembled the two-door Wagoneer, but also managed to siphon away a few sales from the Jeep Universal and Jeepster Commando. The Blazer's available V-8 engines, removable fiberglass top, good ride, and decent off-road ability allowed it to steal sales from across the Jeep product line.

Bring on the Seventies

In the 1970s the popularity of Jeeps and Jeep-like vehicles grew even more. For young people, the musclecars so popular in the 1960s had grown more expensive to insure, and emissions regulations had emasculated once-powerful engines. Many sought automotive thrills in other areas. Four-wheeling was fun, didn't necessarily require a powerful engine, and could be done in vehicles that cost no more than the average automobile, sometimes less (which a buyer of a late twentieth century sport utility vehicle will find hard to believe).

Even as the truck and utility market was growing, however, Kaiser Industries was contemplating a retrenchment back to its core group of businesses. The far-flung Kaiser empire included Kaiser Steel, Kaiser Aluminum & Chemical, and other heavy industries that focused on shipbuilding and the like. Big as the company was, though, it was no

The CJ-7 was the first Universal to offer the one-piece hardtop and full metal doors. When the Levis option was ordered, the Jeep received "denim vinyl" upholstery and a Levis logo on the fender, just like on a new pair of blue jeans.

giant in the auto industry, with relatively meager Jeep sales and a scattered dealer body. Most Jeep vehicles were senior citizens, measured in car years. Modernizing would cost a substantial amount of money. Selling the division for the cash it might bring seemed a prudent option.

Among potential suitors, American Motors Corporation proved the most likely, having no line

In 1971 AMC placed its military and postal Jeep business into a separate division, AM General. The two-wheel-drive AM General postal Jeeps, like this 1979 DJ-5G, were outfitted with a metal cab with dual sliding doors, right-hand steering, and a unique five-slotted grille. They were 133 inches long, 63.5 inches wide, and 70.5 inches tall.

The Renegade package added $899 to the price of the CJ-7's $6,445 base price in 1980. The hardtop was another $676. Like most CJs, the vehicle shown has been fitted with aftermarket wheels.

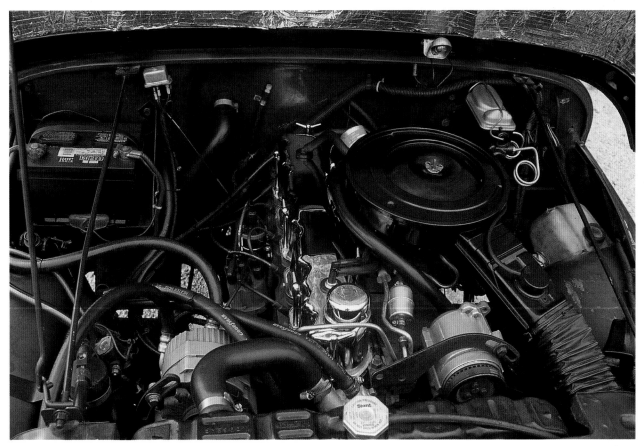

Although four-cylinder engines and V-8s have been available off-and-on throughout the Jeep's life, the workhorse of modern times has been the AMC inline six-cylinder. Besides good torque and economy, the inline six is relatively easy to work on, and is a good fit in the CJ series. The 1980 258-ci six, pictured here with aftermarket chrome valve cover, was rated at 110 net horsepower. The 1990s counterpart, after years of massaging by Chrysler, approaches 200 horsepower.

of trucks or utility vehicles of its own. AMC chairman Roy D. Chapin Jr. was a strong advocate of bringing Jeep into the AMC family. He believed AMC could use the Jeep division to capitalize on the growth in the truck and utility market. Others in the company weren't so sure, but in the end Chapin's views won out. Kaiser sold the Jeep division to AMC in 1970. AMC paid cash and shares of stock to Kaiser, worth somewhere north of $70 million. Kaiser, one of the last of the American automotive independents, later sold its holdings in AMC, thereby quietly exiting from the auto industry.

For AMC, the acquisition of Jeep was a huge boon. The Jeep name was one of the most recognized nameplates in the world, with a proven sales record overseas. The company would immediately be able to tackle Ford, GM, and Chrysler in the growing domestic truck market. And Jeep was

consistently profitable, which would help stabilize AMC's often-shaky bottom line. For Jeep customers, AMC had a larger dealer network than Kaiser, even if that dealer body wasn't always held in the highest regard.

It would take a couple of years to implement, but AMC started planning how it would put its own mark on the Jeep. One of the first changes needed was the replacement of Kaiser Jeep engines with AMC powerplants. Kaiser's engine lineup in the late 1960s was a curious mix of ancient Willys engines and off-the-shelf powerplants from other automakers. AMC had its own line of six- and eight-cylinder engines that would work fine under Jeep hoods.

Another early American Motors' strategy for Jeep included spinning off the military and government side of the business into a new division, AM General. All postal Jeeps, buses, and Army Jeeps would henceforth issue from AM General,

The Levis interior made its debut in 1975, the better to keep a generation of twenty-somethings in familiar surroundings. The Levis association was later dropped, and the option was named simply the "Denim Vinyl" seats. Shown is the 1980 version of Denim Vinyl.

while AMC kept civilian Jeep production separate at the Toledo, Ohio, facility. AM General set up shop in 1971 in South Bend, Indiana, at the former Studebaker plant.

Regardless of these changes, AMC was careful to guard the image of the Jeep. Early AMC advertising in December 1970 bragged "This stubborn runt holds its ground anywhere. It's got Jeep guts. . . . Don't be afraid. Drive it into the ground. Jeep guts can take it."

AMC also continued the strategy of producing special Jeep models. One of the last moves by Kaiser was the production of a limited run of "Renegade I" CJ-5s. The Renegade came with a roll bar, rear-mounted spare, Renegade stripes, ammeter and electric oil gauge, and V-6 engine. For 1971 the series continued with a Renegade II.

AMC kept the Renegade alive for 1972, but with a huge difference—the addition of a V-8 engine. AMC's 304-ci V-8 was equipped with a two-barrel carburetor, and ran an 8.4:1 compression ratio. It produced 150 net horsepower and 245 foot-pounds of torque. By comparison, the single-barrel 232 in-line six produced 100 horsepower and 185 foot-pounds of torque. The 304 was also optional in lesser Jeep models. Joining the standard 232 six and 304 V-8 was an optional 110-horsepower 258-ci six. It produced 195 foot-pounds of torque.

Other Renegade equipment that year included slotted aluminum mag wheels with H78x15 whitewall tires, a "blackout" hood, roll bar, vinyl wheel lips, a Trac-Lok differential, dual mirrors and visors, gas tank skid plate, "Deluxe" upholstery, and a wheel lock for the rear-mounted spare.

The three colors available were called Renegade Yellow, Renegade Plum, and Renegade Orange.

A V-8 in the compact, short-wheelbase CJ-5 was really a case of excess, but competitive pressures were pushing all such utility models in that direction. Ford had equipped the Bronco with its 289-ci V-8 shortly after introduction, and International had even fitted the Scout with a 266-ci V-8 in late 1966.

Of course, "too much" engine is often what gives a car a distinct personality, and makes it collectible in future years. Such is the case with the V-8 Renegades, considered extremely desirable by Jeep enthusiasts.

In 1972 AMC expended some engineering capital in other areas to improve the CJ, although there weren't many external clues that anything had changed. To accommodate the new engine lineup, the CJs were given a stretched wheelbase, from 81 inches to 84 inches. The overall length increased as well, although the new frame on the 1972-1975 CJs later proved less durable than was expected. New springs and shock locations gave these models a slightly better ride. The respected Spicer Model 20 transfer case replaced the Model 18 unit.

Meanwhile, the special editions and sport models just kept rolling forth. The next special edition to arrive was sold alongside the Renegade in 1973. Named the Super Jeep, this edition came

The CJ-7's production run lasted from 1976 to 1986. With its longer wheelbase and larger door opening, the CJ-7 was a more livable package for everyday driving than the shorter CJ-5, although the CJ-5's smaller dimensions were helpful in many off-road situations.

with even wilder stripes across the hood and sides, plus white painted wheels. After astutely noticing how blue jeans had seemingly become the mandatory uniforms of America's youth, AMC offered an optional Levis package in 1975. This gave the CJ denim-like vinyl upholstery and matching canvas top, although the historical record indicating if

Jeep Experimentals

Like every automaker, the "movers and shakers" behind Jeep sometimes feel the need to throw concept vehicles against the wall to see what sticks. Sometimes these concepts are dead ringers for production cars, as was the case with the Concept 1 of the late 1980s, which turned out to be an undisguised Grand Cherokee.

Other efforts were not so successful. In 1969, eyeing a wave of dune buggy popularity, Kaiser put the 1969 XJ-001 on the show circuit. Although built on a CJ chassis, the XJ-001 tossed aside ties to Jeep's past. The fiberglass-bodied two-seater had the look of a sports car/dune buggy hybrid. Apparently the fates frowned on such a coupling, as the XJ-001 was later destroyed when the truck in which it was riding flipped over.

A more serious concept arrived in response to the first Arab oil embargo and fuel crisis. The Jeep II was a 1977 proposal from AMC. The vehicle's mission was fuel economy. The Jeep II was 2 feet shorter than the CJ-5, lighter, and rode lower to the ground. The styling behind the Jeep II was more mindful of traditional Jeeps, even bringing back the flat fenders of the immediate postwar CJ's. But the shrunken CJ never saw production.

Chrysler flirted with the idea of a convertible two-door Cherokee in 1990 called the Freedom. Although as visually exciting as any convertible, Dodge's recent less-than-pleasant experience with its Dodge Dakota convertible no doubt contributed to the quiet disappearance of the Freedom.

Although the Wrangler has sold in greater numbers in recent years, the CJ-5 and CJ-7 have traditionally attracted the greatest number of hard-core enthusiasts. This popularity is reflected in resale values for CJs, which are still among the highest, considering the age and abuse most CJs have been put through

these seat covers were cut from bell-bottom or peg leg sheets of vinyl is, sadly, missing. Levis-equipped Jeeps received a small Levis emblem on the fenders. (Fortunately, AMC failed to take the next step and affix the vehicles with CJ-501 emblems.) The Levis package was available in blue or tan, and was optional on all CJs and standard on the Renegade.

These special editions and option packages were partly to keep the public interested in Jeep's aging product line. In that sense, the tactic worked. In the 1970s, automotive fashion, at least the fashions aimed at youthful buyers, leaned toward loud stripes and bright color schemes. Pontiac's famous Trans-Am, Ford's Mustang II and Cobra II, and even AMC's Spirit-based AMX relied on yards of tape stripes to make their point. With Jeep chasing after the same buyers, it seemed the thing to do.

The Ultimate CJ

The Jeep CJ series arguably reached its peak with the introduction of the CJ-7 in 1976. A well-balanced package, the CJ-7 offered all the traditional strengths and advantages of past CJs but in a more livable and safer package. The CJ-7 rode on a longer 93.5-inch wheelbase, and had larger door openings. The extra length aided the Jeep's on-road handling and made for a more comfortable

The Laredo package joined the CJ range in 1980. This top-line option came with a chrome grille face, high-back bucket seats, and Laredo stripes and decals. When the CJ-7 Limited came along in 1982, it knocked the Laredo off the top spot of the pecking order, but the Laredo survived as a separate model for the rest of the CJ's life, even making a jump onto the YJ Wrangler series.

Leaf springs and solid axles have been a staple of the Universal-type Jeep up until the current Wrangler. Although the suspension isn't the smoothest riding, the hardware is rugged and simple to work on. Diamond plate body panels have gained popularity as a way to cover body damage or to reinforce vulnerable sheet metal.

driving environment. Both the CJ-7 and the CJ-5 benefited from a reinforced frame for 1976.

Thanks to the extra length and widened frame, the CJ-7 could be ordered with an automatic transmission and Jeep's Quadra-Trac four-wheel-drive system. Quadra-Trac was a full-time four-wheel-drive system that first appeared on the 1973 model Wagoneers.

In the mid- and late 1970s AMC paid more attention to customer demands for comfort and

convenience items on its four-wheel-drive machines. The new CJ-7 offered an optional one-piece molded plastic removable hardtop and steel doors with roll-up windows. In 1977 the CJ-series was given a power front disc brakes option, and factory air conditioning was made available on all but four-cylinder models. All CJs were blessed with an improved heating system.

Yet more special editions were introduced. The patriotic theme of the Golden Eagle just missed the American Bicentennial, arriving in the market in 1977. Its equipment included gold wheels, gold pinstripes, a hardtop with tinted windows, fender flares, and an eagle decal on the hood large enough to make a Trans-Am blush. The Golden Eagle package was not cheap, costing buyers more than $1,200. Golden Eagles were available through 1979; in 1980 a Golden Hawk model took its place. There was a special Silver Anniversary CJ-5 in 1979 to celebrate that model's 25 years of production. The Silver Anniversary edition was tied to the Renegade model.

Although the venerable F-head four-cylinder had been retired in U.S. Jeeps after 1971, the Arab oil embargoes and resulting fuel crises in 1973 and 1979, together with the federal government's new Corporate Average Fuel Economy standards, ensured a four-cylinder would find its way back under Jeep hoods. That happened in 1980, when AMC purchased Pontiac's 2.5-liter "Iron Duke" four-cylinder for use in the Jeep.

Sometimes the corporation was working at cross-purposes with itself. During the same period that AMC was attempting to improve Jeep fuel economy, it was also adding luxuries and, therefore, weight. The engineers often chose lighter-duty components and economy gearing as a solution. In 1979, the CJ series was fitted with lighter body panels. In 1981 the 258-ci six was re-engineered in a weight-saving move, losing some 90 pounds in the process.

The ultimate expression of AMC's attempts to create a luxury Jeep was the Limited model, introduced for 1982. *Car and Driver,* in its April 1982 issue, quickly discovered the inherent contradiction of a CJ-7 Limited:

> There seems to be no end to American Motors' efforts to civilize the Jeep. For years now, Jeeps have gravitated from their original no-nonsense, utilitarian origins toward comfort and refinement. But what's the point?

It was easy to understand the puzzlement, as the Limited came standard with the following: carpeting with sound padding and heat insulating material, floor mats, a console, a headliner, chrome bumpers, a "Special Improved Ride Package," padded roll bar, an instrument panel overlay, bright trim rings for the wheels, hood insulation, power disc brakes, power steering, "Limited" stripes, and bodyside steps. *Car and Driver*'s test vehicle even had the optional leather seats and tilt

steering wheel. Although the traditional stout hardware was still there under the skin, it was hard to reconcile the Jeep's utilitarian purpose with the Limited's Cadillac pretensions. Were people truly going to drag muddy boots across plush carpet, settle into leather seats, and go crashing down the Rubicon Trail? Were *that* many people actually comparison shopping the Jeep CJ-7 and the Buick Regal?

Other changes to the CJ series in the early 1980s were more beneficial. The CJ-7 was given a new Borg-Warner T-5 five-speed option. In 1983 AMC introduced its own four-cylinder engine, replacing the Pontiac Iron Duke. The two engines had the same displacement, 2.5 liters, causing some confusion. But AMC's stout four-cylinder proved a good match for the relatively light CJs and the later Wrangler. It produced good torque for a four-cylinder, yet retained good mileage. The 1983 four-cylinder CJ carried EPA fuel economy estimates of 23 miles per gallon city and 28 miles per gallon highway.

AMC made improvements to the 4.2-liter six in 1983 as well, including raising the compression ratio from 8.6:1 to 9.2:1, switching to MCU-Super D electronics, and incorporating a pulse-air injection system in an attempt to improve economy and throttle response.

Wagoneers, Ho!

Meanwhile, many of the strategies that had been employed to keep the CJ current were also used on the Wagoneer. It got its stripes. It got its special editions. It got its fuel economy diet.

But first it got its transfusion of AMC parts. Like the rest of the Jeep lineup, the Wagoneer received AMC V-8 powerplants starting in 1971. AMC's 360-ci V-8 replaced the Buick 350-ci V-8, in use since 1969. In 1972 AMC's 258-ci six was made the Wagoneer's standard engine. AMC's largest-ever bent eight, the 401, was available between 1974 and 1978. It produced a net 235 horsepower, and 320 foot-pounds of torque at 2,800 rpm.

When the Commando was put to sleep after the 1973 model year, AMC quickly introduced a replacement. Much of the action in the utility market was shifting toward the full-size end of the spectrum. Chevrolet's Blazer and GMC's Jimmy had proven increasingly popular, and Dodge was gearing up for the 1974 introduction of its Ramcharger utility. AMC responded with the two-door Cherokee in 1974.

From Bottom to Top— the Expedición de las Americas

The Jeep entered life as a world traveler, being sent to fight on the many fronts of World War II almost as soon as the first Jeep rolled off the assembly line. After the war, Jeeps were assembled in a variety of countries, notably Brazil, Japan, and India. So to see a Jeep in some less-traveled part of the world is no great shock.

Nevertheless, some Jeep treks to the far places are worth noting. One of the more remarkable Jeep tours of duty was logged in 1978 and 1979. Rubicon Trail veteran Mark Smith and other Jeepers Jamboree die-hards assembled a team of CJ-7s to traverse the length of South America and North America. The 21,000-mile adventure, named the Expedición de las Americas, took five months. The Jeepers started north from Tierra del Fuego on December 4, 1978, and arrived in Prudhoe Bay, Alaska, on April 12, 1979. And then they drove home. All Jeeps arrived in one piece.

Mark Smith's Expedición de las Americas 1978 CJ-7 sits in well-deserved retirement in the Jeepers Jamboree collection in Georgetown, California. The vehicle was part of a caravan that traversed the Americas from the tip of Tierra del Fuego in South America to Prudhoe Bay, Alaska.

Why go through all that trouble? Why not? For Mark Smith it was the mountain climbers' credo ringing in his heart: because it's there. Much of the appeal of the trip for Smith was the chance to cross the Darien Gap, a swampy, near-impenetrable section of jungle in Colombia and Panama. The Gap had never been driven overland until 1972, when the British Army managed the feat. It took the Brits 100 days and 250 men. They used race car drivers to pilot the vehicles. Not all of the Colombians who went along made it back.

Smith was convinced a small private group using only Jeeps and muscle could accomplish the feat.

Easier said than done, naturally, and the group nearly gave up on the idea more than once. In 1976 four of the group traveled to Panama to scout the northern end of the route, and came home quite discouraged. They gave the idea one more chance, traveling to Colombia in 1977 to scout the route from the south end. This time they saw things that made them much more confident in the proposed endeavor.

The planning of the journey began. The Darien "conquistadors" included Smith, Ken Collins, Mike and Ken Arnold, Stuart Asbjornisen, Mike Averbeck, Chip Gash, Bob Goodpasture, Al Grim, Bob Renier, Fred Robie, Tim Stigen, Bob Toren, and James Wageman. Three Colombians, Tony Alphonso, Carlos Martinez, and Leon Rendon, were crucial in providing logistic support. Twenty-five Indians were enlisted to help make the crossing.

To begin the expedition, five new CJ-7s were shipped from Long Beach, California, to San Antonio, Chile. From there the crew drove south to Tierra del Fuego, then back north through Argentina. Along the way they passed through Santiago and Ushuaia, Chile; Lima, Peru; Bogota, Colombia; Mexico City; and the United States. They passed through Whitehorse, in the Yukon Territory, and on into Alaska. And right in the middle of it all was the Darien Gap.

The Darien Gap crossing was made possible largely due to sets of interlocking ladders the team had had constructed especially for the trip. The ladders allowed the Jeeps to cross ravines, creek beds, and swampy areas that would have

Mark Smith, a driving force behind the Jeepers Jamboree over the Rubicon Trail, has been a part of the Jeep scene from the beginning. Through such activities as the Jamboree and his Expedicion de las Americas, he has worked with representatives from Willys, Kaiser, and AMC, and as a consultant for Chrysler.

been impassable otherwise. "Of course, the Darien grows at the rate of about 3 feet a month, and that's from the ground up and the top down. By the time we got to one end, our trail was completely obliterated on the other end," Smith said. Of the five months spent on the trip, an entire month was spent crossing the Darien Gap. They often averaged 2 or 3 miles per day. It was a hell of an expedition.

The successful expedition turned out to be a shrewd business move for Smith as well. Already known in Jeep circles for his Jeepmaster role on the Rubicon Trail, the Expedicion de las Americas cemented his reputation. Smith was hired as a consultant for Jeep. Through the years he has helped launch new Jeep models, gotten Jeep on board as a sponsor of the Jeep Jamboree USA series, and even built an off-road test track for Chrysler.

On the face of it, the Cherokee was really just a two-door Wagoneer, but since two-door Wagoneers had been missing from the lineup since Kaiser dropped them after the 1968 model year, it was a welcome addition. The Cherokee was positioned as a less-expensive, sporty alternative to its cushy, family-oriented sibling. It used the J-series truck grille in place of the Wagoneer's busier grille. The 258 258-ci six was standard. The Cherokee was available in S or Sport trim.

The Cherokee line was expanded throughout the 1970s. In 1975 the Cherokee Chief model was added. It included stripes and "Cherokee Chief" identification, but also wider wheel cutouts to allow for larger wheels and tires. The Cherokee strategy proved effective enough that a four-door Cherokee model was added in 1977.

As with the CJ-7, the flamboyant Golden Eagle package and its attendant hood decal was also available on the Cherokee in the late 1970s. The Golden Hawk package replaced it in 1980, with an altered bird design.

The Wagoneer moved into Cadillac territory in 1978 with the release of the Wagoneer Limited. A far cry from earlier Jeep station wagons, the Limited came standard with leather upholstery, an AM/FM/CB stereo radio, and air conditioning.

It wasn't all just tape stripes and power assists in the 1970s, however. There were important upgrades in the Cherokee and Wagoneer's hardware. Borg-Warner's Quadra-Trac automatic full-time four-wheel-drive system made its debut in the Wagoneer in 1973. Quadra-Trac used a controlled-slip differential to allow the vehicle to be run in four-wheel drive no matter the road surface. The Quadra-Trac was standard equipment when the 360-ci V-8 and automatic transmission were chosen.

There were other upgrades as well. The Wagoneer was fitted with a vastly superior Saginaw power steering system for 1974. Like the CJ-5 and CJ-7, the Wagoneers and Cherokees were given strengthened frames for 1976.

Not so Good Times

The American auto industry has seen few years like 1978. U.S. passenger car production hit 9,176,635 units. Truck and bus production totaled 3,722,567. It was the fattest of fat times.

The American auto industry has also seen few years like 1980. Or 1981. Or 1982. From the giddy heights of 1978, total U.S. automobile

Jeep produced a special "Jamboree" CJ-7 in 1982 to commemorate the 30th anniversary of the Jeepers Jamboree over the Rubicon Trail. Only 2,500 were built, all with Topaz Gold metallic paint. This special edition came with a numbered commemorative plaque on the dash.

production plummeted to 5,073,496 in 1982. Truck production had actually bottomed out earlier, in 1980, at 1,634,335 units. A second fuel crisis, a demoralizing hostage crisis in Iran, and high interest rates combined with inflation had dragged the nation into a prolonged economic recession.

The recession crippled every automaker. Chrysler got the headlines for showing up at the Capitol, hat in hand, begging for loans, but other American automakers nearly went under too. Ford was losing $1 billion a year in the early 1980s. AMC and Jeep suffered huge dips in sales. Jeep's U.S. retail sales in 1980 were half what they had been in 1979. Sales dropped even lower in 1981.

Assistance to AMC arrived from an unlikely source. In 1980, French automaker Renault bought part of an interest in AMC. As the year progressed, however, and AMC's condition worsened, Renault bought an even larger stake in the company—46 percent. For Renault, buying into AMC gave the company a large dealer network to market its cars in America. Renault had big plans for its upcoming Alliance economy sedan, which was scheduled for production in the United States. Additionally, the partnership gave Renault four-wheel-drive vehicles to sell in Europe. For AMC, the deal meant ready cash at a time when sales were stuck in the mud. To further free up funds, in 1983 AMC/Renault sold AM General to the LTV Corporation for $170 million. AM General later went on to produce the vehicle that ultimately replaced the military Jeep, the HMMWV.

And if the economic trouble wasn't bad enough, the Jeep picked up two new adversaries in the late 1970s and early 1980s—lawyers and journalists. As the Jeep's popularity grew in the 1970s, more people used the CJ-5 for regular transportation. The typical CJ-5 buyer was no longer the backcountry gent primarily interested in crawling down dusty trails. The Jeep was mainstream, popular with young buyers, and more frequently found in urban driving environments. The problem was the CJ-5's short wheelbase and high ground clearance, ideal for off-road situations, guaranteed that the CJ-5 would never handle like a passenger car in everyday driving. As the CJ-5's popularity increased, so did the number of rollovers. At a time when the term "product liability" was

starting to become a household word, there was no way the CJ-5 could avoid the spotlight.

A December 1980 edition of the CBS news show *60 Minutes* investigated the CJ-5's rollover potential, and, later, so did ABC's *20/20*. These shows focused on the CJ-5's tendency to lift its rear tires during tight "J" turns, and on some of the more tragic accidents involving the CJ-5. Many of the accidents involved driver error or alcohol, but the image of unstable Jeeps soon took root in the public's consciousness. Families of many of the victims sued AMC, and consumer groups like Public Citizen pushed for a defect investigation and possible total recall of the CJ-5.

Ultimately, the National Highway Traffic Safety Administration (NHTSA) ruled the vehicles were not defective. And AMC settled some of the suits. But many of the lawsuits outlasted AMC, and spilled over into Chrysler's ownership with Jeep.

The lawsuits and public pressure made an impression. AMC put more emphasis on Jeep safety. A roll bar was made standard equipment on the CJ-5 in 1980, although even the term "roll bar" soon disappeared. "Sport bar" was the new lawyer-approved term. The NHTSA required warning stickers to be affixed to the Jeep and even dealer brochures in the early 1980s advised:

> All Jeep models are multi-purpose 4-wheel drive vehicles with unique design characteristics that make them different than conventional two-wheel drive cars and light trucks. This is especially true of Jeep CJ-5, CJ-7 and Scrambler models with their high ground clearance, short overhang, narrow width and tight turning radius.
>
> These design features provide unique handling abilities off-road. They also mean that Jeep CJ and Scrambler models will perform differently than conventional cars on pavement.

The CJ-5 had survived three decades in the marketplace, filling its role as a useful servant to two generations of Jeep enthusiasts. But the CJ-5 was rapidly growing obsolete, and the American legal and regulatory climate increasingly less friendly with each passing year. The 1960s and 1970s were years of tremendous growth for Jeep, but as the 1980s dawned it was clear a new direction was needed.

6

MODERN TIMES: THE LATEST AND GREATEST JEEPS

The beginning of the modern Jeep era can probably be traced to the introduction of the downsized 1984 XJ Cherokee and Wagoneer in late 1983. Between that event and Chrysler's purchase of AMC/Jeep in 1987, most of the old vehicles were swept aside, replaced by modern, cleaner, safer new-generation Jeeps.

These Jeep can be considered "modern" in that fuel injection slowly worked its magic on Jeep engines, unibody construction replaced body-on-frame designs, lightweight components shaved extra poundage, and safety features were designed in, not added on later. Styling that had survived for decades gave way to designs that more closely reflected the times. These Jeeps sprang from focus groups and intensive market research.

To be sure, not everyone considered these changes progress. Generally, critics pointed out, unibody designs like those used on the new Cherokee were not as durable in off-road situations as body-on-frame construction. And some of the chassis and suspension revisions aimed at making a safer vehicle reduced the Jeep's off-road prowess. And all that technology doesn't come free.

Despite grumbling from critics, Jeep prospered, with the company seeing sales figures only

Most years Wrangler buyers could choose from at least four, sometimes five models, from stripped to struttin'. The Wrangler SE model, shown, first arrived in 1994. Positioned one step above the entry-level "S" model, the SE took the stripper Jeep and added full padding on the sport bar, 15 x 7 styled steel wheels with P215/75 R15 tires, rear bumperettes, a rear fold and tumble seat, and an AM/FM stereo.

The 1984 XJ Cherokee and Wagoneer went into production in June 1983. The new, slimmer unibody Cherokees were available with two doors or four, and either two-wheel drive or four-wheel drive. Engine choices were initially either AMC 2.5-liter four-cylinder or a GM-supplied 2.8-liter V-6. The Cherokee Chief was the sport model. *Jeep photo*

any other utility vehicles on the market, and the face still said "Jeep."

Further setting the XJ Cherokee apart from trucks like the Chevrolet S-10 Blazer and Ford Bronco II was the availability of two four-wheel-drive systems. The new Cherokee and Wagoneer could be ordered with either the shift-on-the-fly Command-Trac system or the Selec-Trac system. Instead of the independent front suspension systems, which were coming into fashion with many automakers, the Cherokee used solid axles front and rear. The XJ's suspension used leaf springs in the rear, coils up front. The standard engine was the AMC 2.5-liter four-cylinder, with the GM-supplied 2.8-liter V-6 optional.

But the XJ was no pretender. It had to earn its stripes on the venerable Rubicon Trail, home to one of the earliest and best-known Jeep events. Mark Smith, the original Jeepmaster of the Jeepers Jamboree, remembered the Cherokee's early trial runs.

dreamed of in earlier times. Jeep completed the jump, which had been building for some years, from specialized vehicle to daily transportation for millions of Americans. Jeeps were no longer even used in the military.

The 1984 Cherokee was the right vehicle at the right time. It was the first compact American four-door sport utility vehicle, and was the top seller in its class until Ford knocked the Cherokee off its perch with the 1990 Explorer. Others had created compact two-door utilities, but the undiscovered need in the market was for a tough, relatively economical four-door.

"Market studies indicate that more than half of the sales of 4WD vehicles by 1985 will be in the compact segment, compared with only two percent in 1978," said Joseph E. Cappy, vice president of the marketing group at the time. (It later turned out that 70 percent of 4WD sales was in the compact segment.)

AMC and partner Renault spent $250 million in creating the XJ utilities. The new Cherokee was 21 inches shorter, 4 inches lower, and 6 inches narrower than the older Wagoneer, and weighed 1,000 pounds less. AMC designers did a good job of maintaining the Jeep family resemblance. The XJ didn't look like

The Jeep logo has been a constant for decades, as has the spring-loaded hood tie-downs, and folding windshield.

The Laredo model was available on the Wrangler from the YJ's introduction in 1987 until 1990 (shown). As the loaded model, the Wrangler Laredo came with such extras as the chrome grille face, bumper-mounted fog lamps, and larger wheels and tires. *Jeep photo*

"The Cherokee came out in 1983, and it was actually probably in 1980 we took the early Cherokee prototype over the Rubicon," he recalled. "It was at this point they (AMC) were starting to consider the Rubicon the ultimate test for Jeep vehicles.

"I think, in a way, with AMC, toward the end, and then Renault with Francois Castaing, there seemed to be more and more interest in the thing (Rubicon Trail)," Smith said. Production of the XJ began in June 1983. The press introduction was held at Borrego Springs, California, later in the year.

Despite all that was new, the XJ Cherokee didn't stray too far from its roots. A 1984 Jeep press release revealed the thinking behind keeping the Cherokee and Wagoneer names. Cappy noted, "Extensive research indicated we should continue with these two nameplates because they have become synonymous with Jeep," he said. "We felt it was important to get public input in the naming process because these are the first new-from-the-ground-up Jeep vehicles in more than 20 years. A name has a lot to do with how a person perceives the product.

"It became evident very quickly that we would have to have two names instead of one," Cappy said. "The people who leaned toward the sporty models favored the name Cherokee, and the people who liked the more formal four-door wagons favored the Wagoneer name. So we will offer Wagoneer as a four-door only, and Cherokee in both two-door and four-door sport versions."

Whatever the name, the press and public were quickly convinced of the XJ's merits. Jeep produced 93,326 XJ Cherokees and nearly 12,000 XJ Wagoneers for 1984. A rapidly improving economy helped matters.

The XJ won "4x4 of the Year" honors from every major off-roading magazine. *Car and Driver*, in its September 1983 issue, remarked:

> We didn't expect much from the four-cylinder; after all, the fours in the Blazer and Bronco do little more than process gasoline into noise. As it turns out, though, the AMC four feels bloody wonderful. This 2.5-liter turns out 100 hp and an incredibly flat torque curve.

As for its off-road prowess, *Car and Driver* concluded, "On a flat-out run through the desert, the Cherokee bobbed along happily, the suspension both resilient and able to soak up 80-mile-per-hour charges through the *vados* of the Anza-Borrego."

Upon testing a Wagoneer Limited model in its February 1984 issue, it said:

> The ride and handling, the traction, are absolutely first-class. The XJ will do whatever a Bronco

Although a unibody design is usually not the favored configuration for heavy off-road use, the XJ Cherokee was a capable trailblazer thanks to live axles front and rear, and Jeep's rugged four-wheel-drive system. Plenty of owners discovered their Cherokees were capable of a lot more than suburban commuting. Compared to its contemporaries, the XJ was arguably the best American compact sport ute in off-highway situations.

or Blazer will do, and it'll do it more comfortably and with a lot less fuss. The XJ has better ground clearance, a better ride, and more wheel travel than its most obvious competitors, and it's a genuine delight in heavy going, truly a low-buck Range Rover.

Later, the magazine expressed reservations about at least one part of its original assessment. After a 30,000-mile long-term test of a 1984 Cherokee Chief, *Car and Driver* had especially soured on the four-cylinder engine, and reliability was found to be pretty average. As the article reported:

What struck the *C/D* team most about the Cherokee was its sluggishness," said the article. "The most frequent complaint in our log-book was that the Chief had no beans—especially on the highway. Fifth gear was useless for anything but holding a constant speed on dead-level terrain. Any hill or passing maneuver required a bothersome downshift—or two.

The four-cylinder produced good torque figures, but was best matched with the lighter CJ Jeeps than the heavier Cherokee. But the overall package was popular, and the XJ Cherokee quickly became the bestseller in the Jeep lineup.

Old Business

As the new Cherokee and Wagoneer were ushered in, several older Jeeps were shown the door. AMC announced that for 1984 it was dropping the full-size two-door Jeep Cherokee, the CJ-7 Limited, and the J-10 Sportside pickup. The old full-size Wagoneer stayed in production, but was renamed the Grand Wagoneer for 1984. It was loaded with comfort and convenience features and positioned further up market.

Most significantly, the venerable CJ-5 was given the axe. The reason given was to "reduce production complexity at Toledo," but most knew the shortest-wheelbase CJ was also dropped because it was a large target in an increasingly litigious society. By then the longer-wheelbase CJ-7 was the more popular of the two, and was less prone to accidental rollovers. And the CJ's replacement was already well along in development.

During the twilight of the CJ-7's life new developments were modest. In 1985, a fold-and-tumble seat replaced the CJ-7's fixed-back rear seat. The Renegade and Laredo got new stripe patterns. Although still beloved by many, the CJ-7 was just marking time.

Even if many on the inside knew the CJ-7 was a lame duck, AMC still created a huge stir when it announced the end of production of the CJ Jeep before making a clear announcement about its replacement. The word went out on November 27, 1985. "Completion of CJ production will signal an end of a very important era in Jeep history," Cappy, then executive vice president-operations, said. "The quarter-ton Jeep earned a worldwide reputation for ruggedness and versatility in wartime. That tradition has continued for more than four decades that the CJ—which stands for civilian Jeep—has been sold to the public." Cappy had reason to brag. More than 1.5 million CJs had been sold since the series' introduction in late 1945.

But there was confusion in the press, and the story was often presented as if it were the end of traditional open Jeeps, period. At the time, the Japanese automakers were gouging out huge chunks of the American market for themselves. Japanese business interests were purchasing many high-profile American properties. The end of the traditional CJ Jeep was lamented as the loss of one more unique part of America's heritage.

Of course AMC had no intention of extinguishing the line of small, soft-top Jeeps. The

The Renegade name was revived in 1991 for a special Wrangler model. The Renegade came standard with wild fender flares with integrated side steps and more traditional bumpers. Although visually striking, the extra bodywork was more hindrance than help in off-road situations. The other big Wrangler news for 1991 was that Chrysler was finally retiring the carbureted 4.2-liter six, and replacing it with the fuel-injected 4.0-liter six. The flared Renegade model was produced from 1991 to 1994.

image generated by a "Universal" type Jeep was too powerful. Ask people around the world to draw a picture of a Jeep and the resulting image would *not* be of some four-door utility wagon. The original Jeep silhouette is unmistakable, and instantly recognized worldwide.

So when the CJ's replacement, the Wrangler, first rolled off the assembly line on March 12, 1986, scheduled for a May introduction as a 1987 model, it looked an awful lot like the vehicle it was supposed to replace. The Wrangler's design mimicked that of the CJ, with wide fenders, cut-down doors, spring-loaded hood latches, and a traditional seven-slot grille. The instantly recognizable feature that distinguished the two was the Wrangler's use of square headlamps, a first for a Universal Jeep.

The Wrangler, known simply as the YJ in Canada, shared much with the recently introduced XJ Cherokee. They both utilized the same transfer case, axles, brakes, steering, wheels, and base four-cylinder engine. Both also shared more crisply folded styling than their immediate predecessors did.

But the Wrangler kept much of the CJ about it, too. The folding windshield returned, and the Wrangler used leaf springs front and rear, whereas

the XJ Cherokee used leafs only in the rear. And the Wrangler certainly did not follow the XJ's lead to unibody construction. The new YJ still was constructed with a body on frame design.

But engineers did ensure the new Jeep would be more in tune with the modern world. The Wrangler had a wider track than the CJ, and lower ground clearance—all of which made for a better handling vehicle on the street, but hampered off-road ability. The interior was much less Spartan than previous Jeeps, with a full-length instrument panel and a bank of gauges. The instruments were still sealed, so if the Wrangler were left open in foul weather nothing vital would be ruined. The canvas top was no longer secured solely with snaps. A channel system located around the perimeter of the body gave the soft-top a better fit. Raising that top was still more like erecting a tent than simply flipping up a traditional convertible roof, but some quirks had to be saved for the next generation to iron out.

The 1987 Wrangler was available in S, Standard, Sport, and Laredo trim. The base price was $9,195. The new Jeep was available with a fuel-injected 2.5-liter four-cylinder, or a carbureted

The Rio Grande model joined the Wrangler lineup during 1995, the last year of YJ production. The package was tied to new Southwestern-style colors, and featured Rio Grande identification, steel spoke wheels, power steering carpeting, and Rio Grande upholstery. *Jeep photo*

4.2-liter six-cylinder. The four actually produced higher horsepower than the six (117 versus 114), although the six obviously produced greater torque (210 foot-pounds versus 135). All Wranglers were equipped with four-wheel drive, and utilized the Command-Trac shift-on-the-fly four-wheel-drive system.

The Wrangler accomplished most of the goals the AMC engineering and marketing teams had set for the vehicle. *Car and Driver* writer Pete Lyons, in an early March 1986 preview, decided:

> The new Jeep retains all of the open-air-fun feeling of old, yet it is a major advance as in such areas as comfort and handling. On pavement it actually corners with some competence; the tippy feeling is gone. But on the pre-production samples, at least, the power steering was too soft and the seats gave too little lateral support for serious driving.

Later, following a June issue driving opportunity, the final verdict was in. *Car and Driver* reported:

> As an off-road vehicle, the new Wrangler has few equals," said *Car and Driver*. "As a pavement pounder, although it has a more well-rounded personality than the CJ, it still has several shortcomings that keep it from being a satisfactory alternative to a conventional passenger car. The Wrangler is both a significant improvement over

and a worthy successor to the CJ, but it's still a vehicle that prefers dirt under its wheels to life in the fast lane.

Although some true believers derided the YJ Wrangler as a "Yuppie Jeep," the public had few qualms. The Wrangler sold as well as the CJ-7 early on, and in 1989 surpassed the CJ-7's best year.

New Owners, Yet Again

The Wrangler represented AMC's last new Jeep. The mid-1980s economic recovery had been slow to reach America's number four automaker. The XJ Cherokee was selling well, and the Wrangler showed great promise, but AMC's automotive side was a tremendous drag on the company. AMC never quite found the right design to carve out a large part of the mainstream automobile market. The glory days of the Rambler gave way to the days of Pacers and Gremlins, Spirits and Eagles. Renault's new small cars were not much help, and the French automaker was looking to unload its American albatross. It was a long, slow slide. AMC had been losing money for a long time.

Chrysler's corporate wallet, on the other hand, was ready to burst. The company had paid back its government loans early, thanks to the success of

Wrangler cut-away reveals the TJ's Quadra-Coil suspension and New Venture 231 Command-Trac transfer case. Changes from years past include driver- and passenger-side air bags, air conditioning integrated in the dash, and a hand-operated emergency brake in place of the foot-operated type. Underhood, the air intake was mounted higher than on the YJ Wrangler, the better to cross deep water. Purists hailed the return of round headlamps. *Jeep photo*

the K-cars. The new minivans launched in 1983 showered the corporation with money. Other new cars, like the Dodge Daytona Turbo, showed a distinct Mopar design sense, and connected well with the public. The company was well positioned for the economic recovery of the 1980s.

Chrysler had already purchased Lamborghini outright and had formed a partnership with Maserati. Chairman Lee Iacocca was actively shopping for more bargains. And as Jeep had helped fill a hole in AMC's lineup in 1970, Jeep could help fill a void in Chrysler's lineup in 1987. Dodge had pickup trucks, vans, and the aging two-door Ramcharger, but no other entries in the growing sport utility field.

Chrysler purchased AMC outright on August 5, 1987, for somewhere between $1.7 billion and $2 billion, depending on how costs were counted. Although the deal included all of AMC's automotive

operations, the only real prize was the Jeep line and a new factory in Canada. Chrysler integrated its new vehicles into a Jeep-Eagle division, with AMC chief Joseph Cappy at the helm, and Francois Castaing heading up engineering. The Eagle line was largely a repository of leftover AMC-Renault automobiles and Chrysler's Mitsubishi imports. The strategy for keeping Eagle around was twofold: to give Jeep dealers automobiles to sell, and to attempt to create a new image that might attract import-leaning buyers. Eagle cars never quite caught on, though, and as the years passed Jeeps were more likely to be found on Chrysler-Plymouth lots. The Eagle division quietly phased out in 1997.

So what did Chrysler inherit? A new, unproven Wrangler, a popular four-year-old Cherokee and Wagoneer line, a recently introduced Comanche pickup, the aging Grand Wagoneer, plus a creaky line of J-10 and J-20 pickups, which were put to sleep immediately.

The best of the bunch, from a business standpoint, was the XJ Cherokee and Wagoneer. The buyer demographics, the sales volume, and the profit margin were exactly what Chrysler coveted. Production had inched closer to 200,000 units annually in the late 1980s, thanks in no small part to a regimen of constant improvement.

In 1985, AMC had supplemented the four-cylinder and V-6 engine choices with an OHC, 2.1-liter turbo diesel four-cylinder option, a benefit of AMC's partnership with Renault. In 1986 the base 2.5-liter four-cylinder exchanged its carburetor for throttle body fuel injection.

One of the biggest improvements was tossing the optional 2.8-liter GM V-6 overboard like the boat anchor it was. A fuel-injected, efficient 4.0-liter

straight six producing 173 horsepower replaced it in 1987. This straight six, which shared much with its 2.5 liter sibling, later became the backbone of the entire Jeep lineup. Another Cherokee upgrade in 1987 was the availability of a new electronically controlled four-speed automatic transmission, developed by Japanese manufacturer Aisin-Warner.

In the late 1980s, Chrysler owned the compact four-door utility market thanks to the Cherokee, even if Chevrolet's two-door S-10 Blazer was the overall segment leader in the compact field. In 1990 the one-millionth Jeep XJ rolled off the Toledo assembly line. The significance was certainly not lost on Chrysler officials. It had taken the CJ series Jeeps 40 years to reach the 1.5 million sale level. The XJ Cherokee had reached production of 1 million vehicles in less than seven years. "While sales are important, we take greater pride in how the XJ has influenced the

Unique Grand Cherokee Laredo equipment included argent lower bodyside cladding with a black accent strip, argent fascias and bumper guards, a bright grille with argent inserts, 15 x 7 five-spoke wheels, and front bucket seats and door panels covered with "Barton/Bishop" cloth. The Laredo occupied the middle ground in the Grand Wagoneer pecking order, between the base and Limited models. *Jeep photo*

The 1997 TJ Wrangler incorporated a number of changes to make the open Jeep more livable. The soft-top could be folded down much like a traditional convertible. The front of the hood was lowered and the windshield slant increased four degrees to improve aerodynamics and reduce wind noise. And the windshield wipers finally lay all the way down to the base of the windshield. *Jeep photo*

evolution of the sport utility buyer," said Martin Levine, general manager of the Jeep/Eagle division of Chrysler. "In the early '80s, sport utility buyers were, for the most part, truck buyers. Today, most Cherokee and Wagoneer buyers consider their Jeep vehicle as an alternative to a passenger car."

The old full-size Grand Wagoneer even proved a source of profit. Its place in the world had changed considerably since its 1962 introduction. *Four Wheeler* magazine's *1988 Light Truck Buyer's Guide* summed up this new alignment. In comparing the Grand Wagoneer and Chevy Suburban, it observed:

The two vehicles don't compete directly, however, because the concepts behind the two trucks are totally different. The Suburban is the working man's big rig. It has power, room and reasonable comfort, and it is designed to haul tools, pull trailers and get construction crews out to the job site.

The Grand Wagoneer, on the other hand, is the gentleman's 4x4, a large, four-wheel drive station wagon for gadding about the country estate in

opulent comfort. This truck has full carpeting, six-way power front seats, extra sound insulation, power windows and door locks and electric outside mirrors.

Who Owns Whom?

Chrysler latched onto the Jeep heritage like the proverbial bulldog. Lee Iacocca appeared in advertisements with ancient Jeeps, assuring the faithful. "We won't fool around with an American Institution. Jeep will stay Jeep. That's a promise," the ads read. Chrysler even embraced the " Jeepiest" of Jeep events, the Jeepers Jamboree over the Rubicon Trail. "We've generally had most of the top brass from Chrysler over the trail, including Iacocca in 1989," Rubicon Jeepmaster Mark Smith said. Smith recalled Iacocca as being particularly astounded at what the Jeeps were capable of. "He said it was the best half-day of his life," Smith recalled. "Bob Lutz (Chrysler President) made the comment that all Jeep vehicles must be capable of the Rubicon Trail," Smith

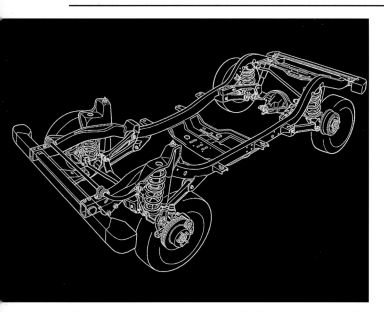

The major improvement of the TJ Wrangler over the YJ was the switch to a coil spring suspension from leaf springs. The TJ's frame was also strengthened, improving torsional stiffness. The coil spring suspension offered greater wheel-to-wheel articulation. *Jeep illustration*

said. Smith later duplicated some of the Rubicon's features at a special Chrysler off-road test track.

But if Chrysler now owned one of the biggest prizes in the auto industry, it also inherited huge expectations. And the success of the Cherokee was beginning to attract its share of imitators. Like AMC in the 1970s, after emptying the vault to purchase Jeep Chrysler had to skimp on new product development for a while, especially with several aging Dodges and Plymouths in need of attention. The recession of the early 1990s further stifled Jeep sales.

Ford struck the biggest blow with the introduction of its four-door (technically five-door, counting the hatch) Explorer. As a utility vehicle, the Explorer offered considerably less off-road ability than the Cherokee, but its middle-of-the-road personality appealed to a great many people. In seemingly no time the Explorer was one of the top-10 selling vehicles in the United States. Chevrolet finally added a four-door model to its S-10 Blazer line in 1991. Nissan and Toyota also expanded their offerings to include four-door models of the Pathfinder and 4-Runner trucks, further challenging the XJ Jeeps.

In place of developing expensive new models, Chrysler kept the existing Jeep line evolving. Gradually, AMC parts were retired and Chrysler

parts phased in. The Wrangler tried to attract customers by offering a variety of different personalities. Wrangler choices expanded for 1988 with the introduction of the Sahara model, and, in 1989, with the Islander. The Sahara was sold in unique Coffee, or Khaki metallic colors, along with color-keyed flares, bumper-mounted fog lamps, matching wheels, a special spare tire cover, and special upholstery and interior trim. The Islander had more of a tropical flair to it thanks to a brighter color selection, and was sold with unique "sundown" stripes, Islander tire cover, and bodyside cladding with side step.

Automobile magazine, in its February 1991 issue, sampled Wranglers from both ends of the spectrum and came down firmly in favor of the simple base model. The magazine ranked the four-cylinder Wrangler S well above a six-cylinder Islander. Regarding the Islander, it judged:

> In the dirt however, our powerhouse became a runaway freight train. Having screamed up the long, rutted hill (pretty much beating the tar out if its occupants) with power to burn, the mighty Jeep didn't have a gear low enough to use engine braking to ease properly down the dangerous slope with the driver's foot clear off the brake pedal . . .

The characteristics of the S model rang more true to *Automobile*. As the article recorded, it was:

> A beautifully balanced four-cylinder engine with perfect gearing," the article recorded. "Plenty of power for its mission, which now has stretched to commuter chores. Without a doubt the standard of measure in this class: flexible, unstoppable. The right granny gear for downhill descents.

More functional improvements for the Wrangler arrived in 1993. That year an anti-lock brake system was added to the option list ABS. The rear of the roll bar was expanded up and outward to the back of the cab. In 1994 CFC-free air conditioning replaced the older a/c system midyear. The 1994 models were recognizable by their new center-high-mounted stoplight peeking over the top of the spare tire.

Chrysler's Turn

Chrysler's opportunity to put its stamp on the Jeep legacy arrived in 1992, although the future Jeep had been in the works for several years. First revealed as the Jeep Concept 1, this proposed successor to the XJ Cherokee had actually been started during AMC's time. Chrysler planners carried the development of the Concept 1 forward for a 1992 launch as a 1993 model.

The Concept 1 showed that, in an about-face from previous thinking, engineers were paying much more attention to the aerodynamics of future sport utilities. The Concept 1 boasted flush glass, and a grille and windshield laid back at fairly extreme angles for a truck. The design team once again performed the neat trick of making a stylish vehicle while maintaining traditional Jeep visual characteristics.

The design was also clearly mindful of the fact that the overall sport utility market was moving upstream, infringing on the turf of luxury car-markers as varied as BMW and Cadillac. The "ZJ" Jeep was larger, had a better ride, and was packed with more luxury features than the XJ. There was room under the hood for a V-8. The new Grand Cherokee would be the first sport utility with a standard driver-side air bag. (The passenger-side bag was added in 1996.)

When the new ZJ Grand Cherokee made its public debut (with Chrysler president Bob Lutz driving one through a plate glass window at the 1992 Detroit auto show), the world discovered the Concept 1 was a virtual production-ready representation of the finished product. Production began in January 1992, as 1993 models, at Chrysler's Jefferson North Assembly Plant in Detroit.

The ZJ was originally planned as a replacement for the XJ Cherokee. But because of the explosive growth in the sport utility market, specifically Ford's success with the Explorer, Chrysler decided to keep the XJ Cherokee in production. The strategy involved using a two-tiered marketing approach, with the two Jeeps bracketing the Explorer. The XJ Cherokee's model range was simplified and the vehicle's accessories limited, allowing its window sticker to undercut that of the Explorer's. Meanwhile, the ZJ was able to stake out the high ground and go toe-to-toe with vehicles like the Eddie Bauer Explorer and Oldsmobile Bravada. The strategy proved remarkably effective, as the market for sport utilities in every price range was quite strong. With the American economy pulling out of recession, XJ sales didn't skip a beat with the introduction of the ZJ.

While larger overall than the XJ Cherokee, the Grand Cherokee still occupied the middle ground

Although the four-door models were more popular, Jeep offered entry-level buyers economical alternatives like the two-door, 2WD Cherokee SE. Shown is the 1998 model. *Jeep photo*

of sport utes. Its wheelbase was 4 inches longer, its overall length 8 inches longer, and its weight 600 pounds heavier than the smaller Cherokee. Although it was a size up from the Cherokee, the Grand Cherokee was no Suburban.

The Grand Wagoneer name was transferred to a top-line ZJ model, which kept the old Grand's wood-sides. Compared to the J-series Grand Wagoneer it replaced, the ZJ's wheelbase was 3 inches shorter, its overall length 10 inches less and, in four-wheel-drive form, its weight nearly 600 pounds trimmer than the luxury encrusted Grand.

The Grand Cherokee made positive strides in handling and off-road ability. Banished from the undercarriage were the traditional Jeep leaf springs, replaced by coil springs at all four wheels. Labeled the Quadra-Coil suspension, the multi-link arrangement nonetheless kept solid axles for maximum toughness. The optional Up Country Suspension gave an additional inch of ground clearance thanks to P235 tires, heavier-duty coil springs and jounce bumpers, high-pressure gas shocks, and styled steel wheels.

Another new addition to the tech sheet was the "Quadra-Trac" four-wheel-drive system. This full-time automatic system required no driver input, but did include a low range for "real" off-roading. Standard on the Grand Cherokee was the

It's hard to imagine what mid-century Willys engineer Barney Roos would have thought of the luxury-soaked Jeeps of the 1990s. In 1998, Jeep released the top-of-the-line Grand Cherokee 5.9 Limited. Underhood was the largest engine seen in a Jeep in a decade. The 5.9-liter (360-ci) Mopar V-8 produced 245 horsepower at 4,000 rpm, and 335 foot-pounds of torque at 2,800 rpm. The 5.9 Limited came with such body-pampering luxuries as heated leather seats, a leather console and door trim, 10-speaker stereo with controls mounted in the steering wheel, and a louvered hood. *Jeep photo*

Command-Trac part-time system, with the shift-on-the-fly Selec-Trac system optional.

The Grand Cherokee was available as a base model, Laredo, or Limited. The base Grand Cherokee engine was the 4.0-liter six, which had been massaged over the years to produce 190 horsepower. Despite the AMC origins of much of the ZJ, the Grand Cherokee was clearly Chrysler's baby. Its optional 5.2-liter V-8 traced its heritage back to the Magnum, Super Commando, and Six-Pack musclecar engines of Mopar's heyday. In fuel-injected form, it produced 220 horsepower and 285 foot-pounds of torque.

The Grand Cherokee's combination of luxury, looks, and class-leading off-road ability helped make it even more popular than the XJ Cherokee. On April 26, 1996, Jeep produced the 1,000,000th Grand Cherokee, a mere four years after the start of production.

Tracing the Grand Cherokee's development through the 1990s has mostly been an exercise in climbing "Mount Upscale." First, there's the Orvis Edition, introduced in 1996. Orvis is a Vermont-based manufacturer of fly-fishing equipment and other sporting goods with an enviable customer profile. Like Ford's Eddie Bauer Explorer, the Orvis Edition Grand Cherokee illustrated perfectly the customer Jeep was trying to reach—wealthy enough to afford high-dollar fishing tackle, mindful of an outdoorsy image, and able to pay for it.

To attract those people, the Orvis Edition included a Moss Green exterior with red and gold stripes; painted 16-inch aluminum wheels; Orvis badging and logos on the floor mats; heated leather seats; and Moss Green, Saddle, and Roan Red interior colors. Other special features included a compact disc player with eight speakers in six locations, automotive temperature control with memory system, and Quadra-Trac 4WD.

Jeep tried to broaden the appeal of the Grand Cherokee to seduce the sports sedan crowd in 1997 with the release of the TSi. Available with either the four-cylinder or six, the TSi emphasized handling with 16-inch Goodyear ES tires on five-spoke aluminum wheels. But it didn't skimp on the luxury, with 10-way leather power seats, steering wheel-mounted stereo controls, and maple woodgrain accents. The TSi naturally had its own identification plates to distinguish it from its other corporate siblings.

Beijing Jeep: We're All Comrades Now

International corporations have long been bewitched by visions of China's 1 billion-plus citizens suddenly throwing off the restraints of communism and driving China's economy into the fellowship of the world's economically elite nations. Naturally, the first thing such newly free and prosperous people would do is buy a car. Or such is the hope.

Automakers from around the world have sought for decades to gain a toehold in the Chinese market. Some assume the communist governing structure will eventually collapse, much as it did in the former Soviet Union and Eastern Europe, and want to be first in line when the world's most populous nation goes on its first shopping binge. Others already have partnerships and alliances with various governments around the globe, and see joint ventures with foreign governments as the normal course of business.

Naturally, it's not that simple. It's impossible for corporations from other nations to simply fly over, build a factory, and start selling cars in China, since the Chinese government picks which companies will set up shop. Its criteria include issues such as job creation, the suitability of proposed vehicles for the Chinese market (a choice not left to the citizenry), capital investment, and especially the opportunity for technology sharing. Usually there is a "corporation" with which foreign companies can form partnerships, but these organizations are little more than a branch of the government.

American Motors was one of the winners of this courtship. A contract between AMC and China forming Beijing Jeep was signed in May 1983. Production of Chinese market Cherokees started in 1984. An all-American icon, Chinese officials also saw the Cherokee as a sort of "people's wagon." Chrysler continued the Beijing operation after its 1987 purchase of AMC.

But Chinese partnerships can also backfire, and badly, as recorded in Jim Mann's book, *Beijing Jeep—The Short, Unhappy Romance of American Business in China*. Hands-across-the-water partnerships are fine and all, but if the Chinese government becomes openly oppressive, it looks bad to be in business with them. Such was the case in 1989. After the Tiananmen Square massacre of Chinese dissidents, many Western corporations with Chinese operations were left to answer tough questions. Chrysler left the country immediately, pulling out all employees. But it returned within a month, unwilling to walk away from a substantial investment. The Beijing Jeep operation continues to this day.

The problem with Chinese joint ventures is that it basically comes down to going into business with a communist dictatorship. Some earnestly believe such partnerships will further the cause of democracy by economically empowering the people of China. Some don't see the Chinese government as a threat, and just hope to benefit from the awakening of a huge future market. And so business rolls on, and conditions change slowly. The vigil for China's anticipated economic awakening continues.

Chrysler created more of a true sports model for 1998. The Grand Cherokee 5.9 Limited packed a much bigger punch than the TSi. With a 245-horsepower 5.9-liter V-8 underhood, the 5.9 Limited reached the upper limit of sport ute performance.

Looking Abroad, Again

The Jeep has always been an international commodity, and as Chrysler continued to integrate the Jeep line into its corporate family, it moved to strengthen that heritage. During Chrysler's near-collapse in the late 1970s and early 1980s, the company had pulled in its overseas arms, either selling off or closing down much of its international operations. As the corporation's fortunes improved in the late 1980s, Chrysler began looking overseas again. The company's tentative steps involved exporting minivans and other select models to countries known to be receptive to American cars, such as the Scandinavian nations.

The Jeep was the perfect vehicle to help Chrysler re-establish itself around the world. It was recognized in every corner of the globe, and therefore had the potential for huge profit in international markets. Beyond that, selling the Jeep overseas was symbolically important to an American auto industry that had watched newer foreign rivals challenge for world domination for years.

Part of Chrysler's international plans for Jeep expanded on AMC's old vision of tapping into the potentially huge Chinese market (see sidebar). But another goal was making headway in a Japanese market notoriously indifferent to American cars. In 1996 Chrysler began producing right-hand-drive Grand Cherokees for the Japanese and United Kingdom markets.

To further emphasize Jeep's global ambitions, the YJ Wrangler's replacement, the TJ, made its debut at the 1996 Tokyo Auto Show, in right-hand steering form. Even though Chrysler's automobiles had had a tough time in the Japanese market, it was hoped a unique vehicle like an updated Jeep could excel.

However, it was government dictates as much as market pressures that drove the TJ's arrival on the scene. Several regulatory deadlines were looming. Upcoming federal requirements mandated passive restraints for both driver and passenger, along with greater side-impact protection. Re-engineering the YJ to include these requirements would have been a colossal pain. And the Wrangler was getting up in years, at least in the hyper-competitive sport utility market. The days of keeping a vehicle on the market for decades largely unchanged, like the CJ-5, were long gone.

And so the TJ Wrangler included driver and passenger air bags integrated into a much more carlike dash. "The instrument panel posed one of our most interesting challenges," said Craig Winn, Jeep platform general manager. "We were not only designing an instrument panel from scratch, but adding two air bags, integrating the HVAC system [Heater, Ventilation, and Air Conditioning], and allowing for the assembly of left- and right-hand-drive versions. Furthermore, we had to maintain a rugged look and a water-resistant capability."

In the quest for greater driver comfort, the TJ was given the "Quadra-Coil" spring suspension design used on the Grand Cherokee, making it the first time a small Jeep relied on anything other than leaf springs. The suspension design didn't just improve the ride, however. The TJ benefited from improved wheel travel and greater articulation from wheel to wheel. The wheel openings were carved out a bit to allow 30x9.5-inch tires from the factory.

As expected, Chrysler didn't radically alter the traditional Jeep looks. Designer Michael Santoro, who had shaped the Chrysler Cirrus and Dodge Stratus, led the way with the TJ Wrangler. Although at a glance it looked much the same as the earlier Wranglers, the TJ adopted such throwback features as the round headlamps. Most of the styling refinements were incorporated to help improve the Wrangler's aerodynamics and noise levels. The leading edge of the hood was dropped and the windshield laid back at a greater angle to smooth the Wrangler's passage through the atmosphere. These changes also helped reduce the ferocious wind buffeting for which soft-top Wranglers were famous. Even the windshield wipers lay obediently down at the base of the windshield.

"We set out to satisfy the wide-ranging needs of customers in more than 100 countries worldwide, some of which view the Wrangler as an entry-level lifestyle vehicle, while others consider it to be a utilitarian vehicle well suited for primitive roads," said Tony Richards, general manager of Jeep and truck business operations at Chrysler.

The 1997 Wrangler kept the body-on-frame construction of earlier Wranglers, along with the carryover 2.5-liter and 4.0-liter engines, with some modest tuning changes. Overall, the Jeep designers and engineers had achieved the difficult task of updating the Wrangler for the twenty-first century without destroying the features that had made it so popular. "The new TJ is as good as any of them," said Jeepers Jamboree honcho Mark Smith.

That tightrope act of refining without diluting was required when the ZJ Grand Cherokee's first revamping came due, for the 1999 model year. The 1999 Grand Cherokee improved upon the ZJ's strengths, while arming it for battle against a host of new sport utility competitors. Designers kept the recognizable styling of the Grand while giving it a more aggressive, aerodynamic face.

The refined 1999 was larger, with more headroom and hip room in the interior. Product planners addressed an old complaint from Grand Cherokee owners by moving the spare tire from an upright position in the cargo area to a hiding place underneath the floor.

Most of the big news was more technical. Debuting in the 1999 Grand Cherokee was Chrysler's first new V-8 since the A-series small-block appeared in 1964. The new 4.7-liter V-8 was Chrysler's first single overhead cam V-8, and it paired a cast-iron block with aluminum heads. Chrysler tossed away a distributor in favor of coil on plug ignition. The engine produced 235 horsepower at 4,800 rpm, and 295 foot-pounds of torque at 3,200 rpm, despite meeting California's Low Emission Vehicle standards. To go with the fresh V-8, Chrysler introduced a new electronically controlled 45RFE transmission. With first and reverse ratios a low 3.00:1, the 45RFE helped keep the Grand Cherokee's off-road reputation intact. Also keeping that reputation polished was the 1999

The first XJ Cherokee Sport was introduced in 1989, and has since become a popular model. In 1997 Chrysler gave the Cherokee a facelift so conservative even hard-core Jeep fans had to take a second look to tell old from new. At the same time engineers improved such areas as interior comfort and ergonomics. Shown is a 1998 Sport.

Grand Cherokee's use of a wider Dana 30 front axle and Dana 44 rear, with optional speed-sensing Vari-Lok differentials.

As was the pattern in the 1990s, Chrysler was hoping for strong sales of the Grand Cherokee overseas to bolster profits. Chrysler had been looking abroad for increased sales, but in 1998 the company was also looking abroad for other reasons.

On May 7, 1998, representatives from Chrysler Corporation and Daimler-Benz announced that the two giants were joining forces, forming Daimler-Chrysler. Although announced as a merger of equals, the company was incorporated in Germany, and observers viewed the Daimler side of the enterprise as having a bit more clout than its new American partner.

Once again, there was a new name over the Jeep door. And irony of all ironies, the vehicle that had once been so instrumental in winning World War II was now part of a German corporation.

On most levels, the merger made sense. With too many automakers having too much production capacity and chasing too few buyers in the 1990s, such consolidations and partnerships usually produced huge gains in efficiency. Combining Daimler-Benz's engineering skill and worldwide exposure with Chrysler's design and marketing strengths made a good match. The two companys' vehicles did not compete directly, so there was little need for massive layoffs or restructuring.

Early indications hint that Daimler-Chrysler will be mindful of Jeep history. Daimler-Chrysler soon announced plans to build a new 1.1 million-square-foot Jeep plant in Toledo, adjacent to the existing Toledo facilities on Stickney Avenue. Production is scheduled to begin in 2001.

"The entire corporation was touched by the outpouring of support displayed by the people of Toledo. With historical roots going back to the early part of this century, the brand-name Jeep always has been and will continue to be synonymous with the city of Toledo," said Daimler-Chrysler co-chairman Robert J. Eaton. The outlook for Jeep over the next 60 years appears to be sound.

APPENDICES

Military Jeep production

Model	Years	Production
Bantam		
Pilot	1940	1
BRC-60	1940	69
BRC-40	1941	2,605
Willys		
Quad	1940	2
MA	1940-1941	1,800
MB	1941-1945	368,714
M38	1950-1951	60,345
M38A1	1951-1963	90,529
Ford		
Pygmy	1940	2
GP	1941	3,550
GPW	1941-45	277,896

Pictured is an M38A1 being readied for convoy duty.
Camp Mabry Military Museum.

Specifications

1945 CJ-2A (produced 1945-49)
wheelbase	80 in.
length	129 7/8 in.
engine	134-ci L-head four-cylinder
horsepower	60 @ 4,000 rpm
torque	106 foot-pounds @ 2,000 rpm

1948 Jeepster (produced 1948-1950)
wheelbase	104 in.
length	174.8 in.
base engine	134.2-ci L-head four-cylinder
horsepower	63 @ 4,000 rpm
torque	105 foot-pounds @ 2,000 rpm

1948 CJ-3A (produced 1948-53)
wheelbase	80 in.
length	129 7/8 in.
base engine	134-ci L-head four-cylinder
horsepower	60 @ 4,000 rpm
torque	106 foot-pounds @ 2,000 rpm

1953 CJ-3B (produced 1953-1966 [in U.S.])
wheelbase	80 in.
length	129 7/8 in.
base engine	134-ci F-head four-cylinder
horsepower	75 @ 4,000 rpm
torque	114 foot-pounds @ 2,000 rpm

1955 CJ-5 (introduced late 1954-1983)
wheelbase	81 in. (1955-1971)
wheelbase	84 in. (1972-1983)
length	135.5 in.
base engine	134-ci. F-head four-cylinder
horsepower	70 @ 4,000 rpm
torque	114 foot-pounds @ 2,000 rpm

1956 CJ-6 (produced 1956-1975)
wheelbase	101 in.
length	155.5 in.
base engine	134-ci. F-head four-cylinder
horsepower	72 @ 4,000 rpm
torque	111 foot-pounds @ 2,200 rpm

Jeepster Commando (produced 1966-1973)
wheelbase	101 in. (1966-1971)
wheelbase	104 in. (1972-1973)
length	168 in. (1966-1971)
length	175 in. (1972-1973)
base engine	134-ci F-head four-cylinder
horsepower	72 @ 4,000 rpm
torque	114 foot-pounds @ 2,000 rpm

CJ-7 (1976-1986)
wheelbase 93.5 in.
length 147.9 in.
base engine 232-ci. inline six-cylinder
horsepower 100 @ 3,600 rpm (net)
torque 185 foot-pounds @ 1,800 rpm

CJ-8 Scrambler (1981-1985)
wheelbase 103.4 in.
length 177.2 in.
base engine 151-ci. OHV four-cylinder
horsepower 82 @ 4,000 rpm (net)
torque 125 foot-pounds @ 2,600 rpm

XJ Cherokee (1984-current)
wheelbase 101.4 in.
length 168.8 in.
base engine 2.5-liter four-cylinder
horsepower 86 @ 3,650 rpm (net)
torque 132 foot-pounds @ 3200 rpm

YJ Wrangler (1987-1995)
wheelbase 93.4 in.
length 153 in.
base engine 2.5-liter OHV four-cylinder
horsepower 117 @ 5,000 rpm (net)
torque 135 foot-pounds @ 3,500 rpm

ZJ Grand Cherokee (1993-1998)
wheelbase 105.9 in.
length 176.5 in.
base engine 4.0-liter OHV inline six
horsepower 190 @ 4,750 rpm (net)
torque 225 foot-pounds @ 4,000 rpm

TJ Wrangler (1997-current)
wheelbase 93.4 in.
length 151.8 in.
base engine 2.5-liter OHV four-cylinder
horsepower 120 @ 5,400 rpm
torque 140 foot-pounds @ 3,500 rpm

Grand Cherokee (1999-current)
wheelbase 105.9 in.
length 181.2 in.
base engine 4.0-liter OHV inline six
horsepower 190 @ 4,750 rpm (net)
torque 225 foot-pounds @ 4,000 rpm

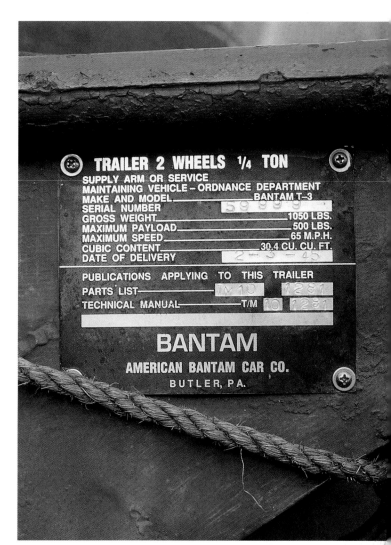

Detail from a World War II American Bantam 1/4-ton Jeep trailer.

INDEX